The Language of Journalism
A Glossary of Print-communications Terms

Ruth Kimball Kent

The Language of Journalism

A Glossary of Print-communications Terms

The Kent State University Press

Illustrations by Bruce W. Kiefer

Library of Congress Card Catalog Number 71–100624
Copyright © 1970 by The Kent State University Press
All rights reserved.
ISBN 0–87338–091–6 (cloth) 0–87338–092–4 (paper)
Manufactured in the United States of America
by Book Graphics, Inc., Evanston, Illinois 60201
Designed by Merald E. Wrolstad.
First Edition

To My Children,
Harold, David, and Grace

Preface

FOR WHOM THE GLOSSARY IS WRITTEN

The purpose of this book is to provide the student of journalism with a handy reference for terms used in his chosen field. Journalism students have a long road to travel. In their years of study, they will have thrown at them a prodigious array of facts, figures, theories, career alternatives, formulas, names, dates, publishing data, tricks of the trade, writing techniques, and a multitude of opinions from instructors and journalists. They will spend long hours at the typewriter, but short hours in the classroom. Instructors are eager to impart an enormous fund of journalistic knowledge, but the task is huge. If bits and pieces of this knowledge can be reduced to clear-cut, authoritative, easily available definitions in one small book, a share of the time students may now spend trying to put these pieces together can be used more profitably in learning more complex data, and, it is hoped, in actual writing.

In fact, the journalism instructor may come to look upon this volume as a teaching aid. It might be a relief to sidestep lengthy explanations by instructing a student to learn a definition from the glossary, then study ramifications in his textbook. Teaching is often a matter of explaining the same thing in more than one way until the student finally has a breakthrough to knowledge. A basic definition may provide a helpful starting point.

The practicing journalist also may find this book of interest. Journalists in our age are specialists, even as their counterparts in other professions. They concentrate narrowly on reporting, research, photography, or any of a dozen other specialties in the field. Yet they come into contact with, and must cooperate with, others in the world of journalism. They find an unfamiliar term cropping up now and then—each specialization develops its own jar-

gon—and a ready source of information might be welcome. Such a source could also serve as a settler of the
inevitable arguments. Then too, the practicing journalist
may be amused by the colorful terms. By trade he is a
wordmonger, and with his flair for language he finds it
natural to invest a commonplace process, tool, method, or
symbol with a lively and colorful designation.

Lexicographers may also welcome a journalism glossary
that has been painstakingly compiled. Many of the sources
for journalism terms now available are hopelessly outdated. Others are compilations of apparently hastily written entries that seem not to be the result of prolonged
study. Still others lack precise formulations; ambiguous
explanatory words have been used in the entries, inviting
misinterpretation. Some use highly technical words within
the entries that could block understanding. Again, some of
the sources are highly specialized, and some are extremely
limited in size as well as scope.

Certain assumptions have been made about the person
who may use the glossary. The first assumption is that he
has a special interest in journalism. The second is that he
has a basic, journalistically-related vocabulary, so there is
no need to provide definitions for broad, generic terms such
as *press, broadcast, newspaper,* or *negative.* Certain other
fairly elementary terms *have* been included, often because
there is one small point that seems worthy of clarifica-
tion—and sometimes in respect for the need for a primary
definition as a jumping-off point.

Another assumption is that the glossary user is a rea-
sonably intelligent being, perhaps even on the sharp, sophisticated side. At least, it seems that working journalists are invariably bright-eyed, alert, and quick-minded,
sometimes to an almost astonishing degree—and perhaps
the student journalist who does not find these attributes
within himself has picked the wrong profession. And so it

is assumed that the journalism student does not balk at big words or technical terms—rather, needs and welcomes them—and doesn't need to be written down to.

FORM OF PRESENTATION

The glossary entries are presented in simple alphabetical order. Compound terms are listed alphabetically according to the first word, as *rotary press*, rather than *press, rotary*. Abbreviations have been given a separate listing, and follow the chapter containing the terms themselves.

DISTRIBUTION OF TERMS

Care has been taken to see that the contents of the glossary are judiciously balanced alphabetically. The middle of the English alphabet, for lexicographical purposes, is judged to be somewhere near LIN. The first quarter is generally hit somewhere in the DIS's. More variation occurs at the three-quarter mark, and there is some disagreement on the ideal—but some lexicographers believe RUM to be a good mark at which to aim. A great many factors can influence distribution, but these rules of thumb are helpful in seeing to it that an alphabetically-arranged reference book is not too full in some sections, but too lean in others.

HYPHENATIONS AND SPELLINGS

Hyphenations and spellings follow what seem to be preferred in the majority of sources. If the choice is close, the alternate is also given. A term used as both noun and adjective (and in some cases, verb) is defined in the form most commonly used. If one sense is as common as the other, both are given, but not labeled as to part of speech. Having the ability to distinguish these is one of the assumptions made about the user of the glossary. Pronunciations are not given except in the double case of the word *lead,* and for *soc.*

GENERAL LEXICOGRAPHICAL PHILOSOPHY

Within the glossary, the use of periods and capital letters may appear to be inconsistent. This seeming inconsistency is a result of reporting actual usage as it seems to be given in the majority of sources or citations from publications.

In each instance where periods or capitalizations are involved, an effort has been made to report usage as it is, rather than prescribing what it "should be." Laying down rules to be used in particular instances lies within the province of a stylebook rather than a glossary.

The same principle has been followed in the chapter containing abbreviations, that is, each is presented in the form that seems to be most commonly used. Some organizations' abbreviations are written with periods, sometimes by choice of the group. Nowadays many are not. When evidence is lacking as to the preferred form, it is given without periods.

However, the philosophy of pure reporting extends only to matters of style and spelling. When it comes to the meanings of terms, this glossary represents a middle-of-the-road lexicographical philosophy. It does not simply report the ways in which words are used without regard for the fact that some usages are regarded as substandard or incorrect. Nor does it maintain a "purist" attitude, and refuse to acknowledge the growth and change of language.

There are some cases in which it does no good to insist that a meaning is "wrong" when common usage by respected writers and serious publications indicates acceptance (sometimes because of lack of a better word). At

other times, a term may appear to be changing and broad-
ening, but is not generally accepted as standard. Yet again,
there are a few terms whose meanings deserve to be de-
fended by lexicographers, with hope of preventing mis-
understanding. A case in point is the erroneous use of
bimonthly to mean *semimonthly*.

SYNONYMS

A preferred term is defined, but its synonyms entered simply, then cross-referred to the preferred term. In some
cases where there are many synonyms, some rare, they are
entered only at the end of the entry for the preferred term.
(See *end paper* or *river*, for example.) For the sake of con-
servation, some entries contain several related terms which
are not then entered separately. These related words are
printed in *italics*.

CROSS-REFERENCES

A fair number of cross-references have been included, in
some cases to save space, but in many more to refer the
glossary user to more information. HALFTONE, for example, has been cross-referred to SCREEN, and there the
explanation of the process is continued, to be further
rounded out at DOT PATTERN. Cross-references are printed
in SMALL CAPITALS.
Entry words within the glossary followed by a star are the
ones whose origins are discussed in Chapter I.

SCOPE

The author of this book does not pretend to present a complete journalism glossary; to compile such would take a lifetime. Also, there is little "new" material. Hardly! A glossary of made-up words would be less than useful. Yet the glossary does contain some journalism terms just now coming into common usage in nonspecialized publications, and not yet in the desk dictionaries of America. (An example is *stringer*.)

While the proportion of "new" words may not be large, it is guaranteed that each entry has been newly formulated, often combining bits and pieces of facts taken from a rather astounding number of sources. It is also a new selection of terms, not previously gathered together in like combination. Many of the terms form no part of daily speech. Many more do form part of daily speech, but have taken on special meanings in the world of journalism. These are journalism terms because they mean more, or at least something more definite, to the journalist than to the ordinary man. Many everyday words, such as *spike, river, box,* or *horse,* have acquired meanings which would be totally unsuspected by the man in the street, and are therefore as worthy of inclusion as *etaoinshrdlu* or *serif*.

The method of research has followed that conventionally used by lexicographers. Essentially, this boils down to looking it up in every source one can find, and consulting the experts. The recording of research has also been painstaking, so that any specific entry, if challenged, can be backed up authoritatively, and not rest solely on the author's say-so.

Although the terms included in this glossary were chosen arbitrarily, the value of each was considered and weighed carefully. Rules for consistency have been followed, including that for entering related terms within a given category. (Examples of this are the terms for each of the major classifications of type, as *roman, italic, sans serif,* etc.). Yet some complete categories have been passed over because the author did not feel qualified to deal with them. (Examples of this are computer terms used in journalistic research.) The alternative to this would have been editing a glossary rather than writing one, and that was not the goal.

What terms have been included?

Mentioned first because it is the author's favorite category, is what may be called journalism jargon. These terms have been searched for far and wide, from the *Oxford English Dictionary* and many such learned works, through the dialect dictionaries and sources dealing only with Americanisms, the specialized glossaries and trade publications, down to the slang dictionaries, which were given a thorough perusal. Perhaps not so much journalism lingo has been gathered together in an exclusively journalistic source before. These terms form the colorful core of the language of journalism, and are generally amusing and interesting to both the general public and the journalist himself.

Then there are the technical or semi-technical terms of journalism, including those that may be used in newspaper, magazine, wire news service, public relations, and advertising.

Included also is a fairly comprehensive selection of graphic arts terms. There are not so many as one would find in the Kingsport Press *Glossary of Technical Terms,* but not so few as one would find in a glossary appended to a textbook.

Along with these are entries for a smattering of terms having to do with paper, book production, the electronic media, statistical research, law of the press, and photography. These fields have been thoroughly and admirably covered in various sources, to which frequent references are made. To duplicate all of these works within one volume would be impossible, so selection was the rule. Names of some journalism organizations have been included, but this selection was necessarily arbitrary, as there are far too many to cover thoroughly.

The abbreviations entered are those which were judged to be those the journalist is most likely to encounter and need to look up. The various stylebooks have fine lists of abbreviations he might need to *use* in his work, such as those for various government agencies, Biblical references, sports terms, or units of weight. These are also included in most desk dictionaries. Therefore, it is not necessary to be all-inclusive and provide these. Rather, it seems important to stick to abbreviations that seem to be peculiar to, or at least related to, the journalism world.

ACKNOWLEDGMENTS

Grateful thanks to those who expressed confidence in me by granting financial aid: to Theta Sigma Phi, for its National Award in 1962; Central New York State Business and Professional Women's Clubs, for a generous grant; Cayuga-Onondaga Presbytery, for the honor of its awards in 1961 and 1962; Syracuse University for honor scholarships; the New York State Scholar Incentive Awards for several semesters; and to my aunt, Miss Evelyn G. Kimball, for providing the balance of my tuition.

Special thanks to David B. Guralnik, editor-in-chief of *Webster's New World Dictionary* and its companion editions, for permission to use the facilities of the World Publishing Company Dictionary Department for research. Yet it must be understood this work was not conducted under the auspices of the Dictionary Department, nor were any of the entries herein "lifted" from the dictionary files nor the dictionary itself. Work on the glossary has not merged with the author's daily work on the dictionary except when it became necessary to reformulate an entry written for the dictionary so it would not be the same in the glossary. At times, it was a challenge.

My deep appreciation goes to Professor Roland E. Wolseley, chairman of the Magazine Department, School of Journalism, Syracuse University. His constant encouragement and splendid example are the inspiration of my life. I am grateful to Professor Catherine Covert (Stepanek), Professor Robert S. Laubach, and Professor D. Wayne Rowland for their careful reading of the manuscript, and their valuable suggestions. Professor Edmund C. Arnold, chairman of the Graphic Arts Department, has kindly answered questions. Thanks, too, to Mr. C. Howard Allen, director of The Kent State University Press.

Two kings and a queen also receive royal shares of gratitude. My son, Harold T. Kent Jr., graduate of San Francisco State College Journalism School, now with the San Francisco Bureau of United Press International, has written me reams of information about wire services and journalism lingo. My second son, Captain David A. Kent, USAF, graduate of Rensselaer Polytechnic Institute, now in North Truro, Massachusetts, with the 762nd Radar Squadron, has provided an endless supply of research material and citations. Daughter Grace Kent Osterlund, graduate of Kent State University, has offered astute editorial opinions as the work progressed.

All responsibility for errors, omissions, inaccuracies, or any kind of poor workmanship rests entirely on me. Formulation of each entry was mine alone.

My last word of thanks goes to Miss Virginia Becker, for her invaluable aid in typing the manuscript.

R.K.K.

May 1969

Contents

I. The Language of Journalism and Its Origins

A. INTRODUCTION

Does the world of journalism need the up-to-date glossary of terms here presented? The answer is yes, for there is not a comparable book readily available to the journalism student. He may look in a great number of sources to find the separate parts of what has been put together and presented here. The importance of journalism, and the education to prepare for a life devoted to it, is vital in our day. At the time of this writing, there are nearly 25,000 students enrolled in 118 schools and departments of journalism across the land,[1] and they need whatever aids can be offered by those interested and versed in the field. James Reston, Washington correspondent for *The New York Times*, says, "The nineteenth century was the era of the novelist. The twentieth is the era of the journalist,"[2] and the pertinence of his statement is hard to deny.

What words does the glossary contain? Attention has been confined to the terminology of print journalism, with a few side excursions. The world of the electronic media is a separate field in itself, and needs a book of its own. In fact, it has one that is fairly comprehensive in Jacobson's *Mass Communications Dictionary*.

What is journalism? As recently as 1945, the *Encyclopaedia Britannica's* entry for *Journalism* had an opening paragraph that can only be described as quaint:

Though the qualifications and status of Clergymen, Physicians and members of many other professions are definite, the Journalist continues to follow an indeterminate calling with neither qualifications nor status precisely defined. The editor of a great metropolitan newspaper is equally a Journalist with the humblest police reporter; and there are many persons who style themselves Journalists who supplement incomes by writing for newspapers and periodicals.

The Columbia Encyclopedia (p. 1098) does little better: "*Journalism*. The collection and periodical publishing of news. It includes writing for, editing, and managing such media as the newspaper and the periodical. . . ."

The entries for *Journalism* in later editions of *Britannica* (1957 and 1967), are more up-to-date:

Journalism includes the writing and editing of newspapers and periodicals. Although this is the basic definition, various tasks and processes intimately connected with the production of serial publications are commonly classified as journalistic. Thus the gathering and transmission of news, business management of journals, and advertising in all its phases are often thought of as coming within the field of journalism. And following the advent of radio and television, there was a trend toward including all communication dealing with current affairs in the term. . . .

The more modern *Webster's New International Dictionary, Third Edition,* calls journalism "the collection and editing of material of current interest for presentation through the media of newspapers, magazines, newsreels, radio, or television. . . ." It seems fair enough for a beginning, though the day of the newsreel is waning.

It is plain to see that *journalism* has a different meaning in the age of mass communications from what it did in the day when "journalist" was synonymous with "newspaperman," and no nonsense about it. Having Nellie Bly insist that it be expanded also to mean "newspaperwoman" was only the beginning. During the past decade one chapter after another of Theta Sigma Phi, the national journalism honor sorority, has voted that the sisterhood be enlarged to welcome radio and television personnel—as a sequel to the preceding years when those in public relations and advertising were liksewise brought into the journalistic family.

Yes, the field has broadened. Photojournalism, communications research, and the electronic media have come into their own. A journalist may be involved in production schedules for a TV documentary, or a journalist may do sociological research for an in-depth feature on the repercussions of yesterday's political decisions. Sometimes it is hard to determine where sociology ends and journalism begins—or politics and journalism—or economics and journalism—or any of a dozen other combinations. Actually, journalism encroaches on them all, for mankind's exploration of any field of knowledge or endeavor is of little value unless the results are written down.

Yet, for all of this, the principal province of the journalist is news. Here the word is used in its broadest sense—information that's new, or presented in a new way—something that has not been told before. Not only the new happenings or events of the world, but a new way to cook a roast, a new approach to a community problem, or a new way of thinking about a religious doctrine. Whatever the information may be, the emphasis is always upon a presentation of that which is new to the reader.

The electronic media may appear to bypass the printed word, but the reams of copy in the studios of the land and the use of TelePrompters assure us this is not so. The news reports given on radio and television are often read verbatim from copy teletyped to the studios from the wire services.[3]

MacDougall, in discussing "Journalism Today and Tomorrow," says:

No matter what electronic devices are developed for the use of the communicator, the need for a permanent record will persist. . . . Whatever the future may bring, as of today the daily newspaper still provides the best basic training for beginners in journalism, no matter what their lifetime ambitions may be. No other medium comes anywhere close to duplicating its efforts at speedy, accurate and thorough coverage of the news of the world. . . .[4]

The influence of the newspaper is enormous, and its readership is huge. The combined circulation of America's 1,754 daily newspapers is 61,397,252.[5] Figures for the weeklies are not as cut-and-dried, but there are about 9,500 non-dailies now being published.[6] It is said that about 150 million Americans read some newspaper every day,[7] and "reader surveys show that most people spend 40 to 45 minutes a day reading the newspaper."[8] Papers vary in size from the Cleveland *Plain Dealer* in its 274-page Sunday glory,[9] to the beautiful 18-page Oberlin (Ohio) *News-Tribune*,[10] an offset weekly with photos fine enough to frame.

These figures attest that the newspaper provides the broad underlying basis upon which the family of journalism rests. Therefore, much of the language that is peculiar to our profession has had its beginning in some part of the newspaper world. Furthermore, the newspaper's primary alliance with the printing press contributes another basis to the broad range of the language of journalism. The copyboy was rushing copy to the compositor in "short takes" decades before the movie cameraman fell into the habit of calling his short sections of film "takes." When the President calls a "press" conference, he talks to the ladies and gentlemen of radio, television, and magazines, as well as those from newspapers—yet the term is primarily theirs. When a radio or television newscaster speaks of his "headlines for tonight" or the "cover story," he is borrowing his words from Ye Olde Gazette.

B. ORIGINS OF SOME JOURNALISM TERMS

The world of journalism has contributed a great many words to our language, sometimes directly and sometimes obliquely. Americans had no dainty, discreet, and glamorous word for women's underwear until Sarah Josepha Hale appropriated *lingerie* from the French language to use in *Godey's Lady's Book.* When Gelett Burgess coined BLURB[11] in 1907, he explicitly said it meant "to sound like a publisher."[12] When someone is cautioned to mind his p's and q's, the speaker is echoing the printer who warns that the types for these characters are easily mistaken for one another,[13] and when a person is "out of sorts," he has only run out of the types for certain letters in a font, a condition to make any printer feel fractious. Yet the journalistic field has also borrowed a great many words from other pursuits and places and made them its own. BALLYHOO, for sensational propaganda or advertising, came almost whole from the town of Ballyhooly, in County Cork, Ireland.

Some journalism terms are easily understood without much explanation. It is easy to see why the trademark MONOTYPE was given to a typecasting machine that casts a single character at a time, while the trademark LINOTYPE designates one that casts a complete line of type. And it is not hard to figure out the derivation of DUOTONE, meaning a print with two color tones. Several words are understood more easily if it is known that LOGO- comes from the Greek *logos,* word, and that PHOTO- is from the Greek *phōtos,* light.

Even with a little thought, others are not quite so obvious because their component parts are not so commonly known: JOURNAL came ultimately from the Latin *diurnalis,* daily, which came from *dies,* day; FACSIMILE is from the Latin *fac,* imperative of *facere,* to make, and *simile,* like; COLLOTYPE is from the Greek *kolla,* glue, plus *type;* INTAGLIO from *in* and the Italian *tagliare,* to cut; and XEROGRAPHY from the Greek *xēros,* dry, plus *-graphy,* from the Greek *graphein,* to write. The *dandy* in DANDY-ROLL originally meant convenient or small— actually, *handy* with a dialectal *d* in front of it.

BRAYER is from *breier,* a Middle English verb meaning to pound or crush; TYPE is ultimately from the old Greek *typtein,* to beat or strike; FLONG came through the French from Late Latin *flado,* a flat cake; and FRISKET is also from French (Middle French) for flirtatious, as a mask should be, and is related to the same sources as those for *frisky* or *fresh.*

SERIF is from the Dutch *schreef,* line or stroke, ultimately from Latin *scribere,* to write, and FONT is from the same Latin base as *found,* to cast (type). REAM came a long way through Middle English and Old French from the Arabic *rizmah,* a packet or bale, and another Arabic term *makhzan,* a storehouse or granary, finally turned into MAGAZINE.

TUSCHE is a back-formation from the German word *tuschen,* to lay on ink or color, from the French *toucher,* to touch. REGLET came through the French from the Latin *regula* for a straight piece of wood (hence RULE), while MACKLE came more directly from the Latin *macula,* spot or stain.

The word GAZETTE, meaning newspaper, came from a newspaper in Venice that sold for a *gazet,* a small copper coin.

But these are only simple etymologies. What of some of the more complex terms in journalism?

It is generally agreed that the term FOURTH ESTATE for the world of journalism, or journalists collectively, was first used in England's House of Commons, but who first used it remains a mystery.

In the days of feudalism, there were three estates having specific political powers. The first estate was the clergy (the Lords Spiritual), the second was the nobility (the Lords Temporal), and the third was the bourgeoisie (the Commons).

Thomas Carlyle, writing in 1841, attributed the first use of FOURTH ESTATE, as applied to the press, to the statesman, Edmund Burke. If this were true, it would have been some time between 1766 and 1794, the years during which Burke served in Parliament.

However, at the entry for *estate*, the *Oxford English Dictionary* states in its scholarly and painfully honest fashion,

We have failed to discover confirmation of Carlyle's statement (quot. 1841) attributing to Burke the use of this phrase in the application now current. A correspondent of *Notes and Queries* . . . states that he heard Brougham use it in the House of Commons in 1823 or 1824, and that it was at that time treated as original. . . .

The pertinent OED citations were as follows: "1837 Carlyle *Fr. Rev.* I. vi. v, A Fourth Estate, of Able Editors, springs up. 1841 [Carlyle] *Hero-worship*, Lect. v, Burke said there were three estates in Parliament, but in the Reporters' Gallery . . there sat a fourth Estate more important far than they all."

A different theory is reported by Robert E. Park, who says:

In the eighteenth century the army was sometimes referred to as a "fourth estate," and at least once "the mob" was thus named. Probably Macaulay was the first to give this designation to "the gallery in which the reporters sit," in his essay on Hallam's *Constitutional History* in 1828, though Carlyle in his "Hero as a Man of Letters" ascribes the *bon mot* to Burke. It is not found in Burke's printed works.[14]

CHAPEL is another term whose exact beginning cannot be traced. It is used now to mean "an association of union members in a printshop." Jacobson says, "A very old term in the printing unions. It is believed that the term is derived from the fact that Caxton set up his first printing press in a chapel adjoining Westminster Abbey." This is given credence in the official history of Westminster Abbey, which says:

Caxton, whose father lived in Westminster, . . . first came to set up his printing press within the precincts of the Abbey, where a relation, Richard Caxton, was a monk, in 1476. From then until 1500 he, and later his assistant and successor Wynkyn de Worde, occupied a shop near the Chapter House. It was not until 1482/3 that he took over premises in the Almonry itself and set up his famous sign of the Red Pale there, . . . Another shop later rented by him may have been either under the Chapel of St Edmund or that of St Nicholas, thus giving rise to the well-known term 'chapel' in the printing trade.[15]

The *Oxford English Dictionary* doesn't try to trace the origin of the term CHAPEL, but only defines it:

a. A printer's workshop, a printing-office. b. A meeting or association of the journeymen in a printing-office for promoting and enforcing order among themselves, settling disputes as to price of work, etc. It is presided over by a *father of the chapel* annually elected. Hence *to hold a chapel.*

The definition is considerably outdated. Sense a. is obsolete, and the "association" is no longer confined to journeyman printers.

The *Encyclopaedia Britannica* points out that in the United States the "father of the chapel" is called the chairman, and gives the Caxton origin of the term CHAPEL from a 1716 book. It also offers an alternate, quite implausible, quotation to account for the origin. A Joseph Moxon, in 1683, offered this explanation: "Every Printing-house is by the Custom of Time out of mind, called a Chappel. . . . I suppse this stile was originally conferred upon it . . . for the Books of Divinity that proceeded from a Printing-house. . . ."[16]

So there was a writer 300 years ago wondering where the term originated. The *Oxford English Dictionary* citations run from 1688 to 1879 (note *Britannica's* citation is for an earlier date than that given in the OED—a rarity). But Caxton died in 1491, so the term must have had currency for nearly two centuries before it was recorded in a source that was saved, to be recovered at a later date.

WAYZGOOSE is a quaint old term of English dialect whose origin has been lost. The *Oxford English Dictionary* defines it as "Originally, an annual entertainment given by a master printer for his journeymen and apprentices," and appends the note that it was usually given in August, and "marked the beginning of the season of working by candlelight." OED's first citation is dated 1731. In both the OED and Merriam-Webster's *Third Edition* an alternate spelling, *waygoose,* is given. The term does not appear in the abridged dictionaries.

An apprentice printer or printer's errand boy has been called a PRINTER'S DEVIL for a very long time—since the seventeenth century—but various authorities disagree as to why he is called this. Some, as Arnold, maintain that the designation was related to a common superstitious belief in the early days of printing that the art was somehow Satanic, with weird and perhaps unholy powers accruing to the printer—and thus his helper would be rightfully called a devil. Others are much more prosaic and state rather simply he was called a printer's devil because he was commonly spattered, and by day's end, nearly covered with the black printer's ink. Merriam-Webster's *Third Edition* gives this explanation, apparently influenced by the *Oxford English Dictionary*, which has an appealing 1683 citation: ". . . These Boys do in a Printing-House, commonly black and Dawb themselves: whence the Workmen do Jocosely call them Devils. . . ." Others, as *Webster's New World Dictionary*, do not search out its source. One might surmise that the name came partly because mischievous young boys are often called "devils," and most young boys do tend to be somewhat mischievous.

The origins of the old names of types present an interesting study. Three of the names for smaller sizes reflect a desire to give the type a name that would denote something superior: EXCELSIOR (3 point), BRILLIANT (3½-4 point), and NONPAREIL (French for *unequaled;* 6 point). Several other of the smaller sizes are named for precious stones: GEM (4 point), DIAMOND (4½ point), PEARL (5 point), AGATE and RUBY (5½ point), and EMERALD (6½ point).

According to *The Columbia Encyclopedia,* ENGLISH (14 point), derived its name in this fashion: "One of the type faces used by Caxton is the original Old English type. The size of this type of Caxton's (14 point) is known as English."[17]

MINION (7½ point) is from the French *mignon,* darling or favorite, with MINIONETTE (6½ point) its diminutive. BREVIER (8 point) was given its name because it was often used to print breviaries (prayerbooks) in Belgium and Holland in the sixteenth century. BOURGEOIS (9 point) took the name of the French typefounder who first cast it. LONG PRIMER (10 point) was originally used to print primers, the laymen's prayerbooks, first printed in Latin, then in English, and used to teach children to read. By extension, 18-point type came to be called GREAT PRIMER because it had a similar face, but was larger, and used to print a larger holy book—the Bible, to be exact. This size was sometimes called BIBLE TEXT by the early printers.

The very large CANON (40 point) was so-called from being used to print the canon of the Mass in the large books to be used at the altar. COLUMBIAN (16 point) is apparently exclusively American, and arbitrarily picked as a name for this size of type, though it may have some relationship to the American Columbian printing press. The English called this size of type *Two-Line Brevier* before the point system was devised. The names for MERIDIAN (44 point) and PARAGON (20 point) are like the names for the smallest sizes of type in simply meaning something superior or fine, though both could be traced back further: MERIDIAN from the Latin *medius,* middle, and *dies,* day, the middle or high point of the day, and thus the prime or best; and PARAGON from the Greek *para-,* against, and *akonē,* whetstone, hence Greek *parakonaein,* to test with a whetstone, hence Italian *paragone,* touchstone, and from there into Old French and into English, to mean a model of perfection. For more information regarding type, see entry in glossary for TYPE SIZES.

Among the old terms having to do with type are MAJUSCULE and MINUSCULE, meaning capital and lower case letters. The large rounded, Latin UNCIAL (from the Latin *uncialis,* inch-high) letters were used in transcribing manuscripts between the third and ninth centuries. Gradually through these years a running script of smaller letters developed, and were called MINUSCULES (from the Latin *minusculus,* rather small, diminutive of *minor,* less), to distinguish them from the conventional larger letters. Quite naturally, these then came to be called

MAJUSCULES (from *majusculus,* somewhat larger, diminutive of *major,* more), for these letters were retained to be used as capitals, that is, reserved for the starting letters of sentences and for beginning proper names. While the division seems commonplace today, its evolution took a very long time.

Another common printing term from the Latin is a direction to the printer, STET, literally, let it stand; nothing more than the third person subjunctive of the Latin *stare,* to stand. One more is the name for the inverted v in copy where there is to be an insertion, CARET, literally, there is lacking; from the third person indicative of *carēre,* to lack or be without.

In moving on to more modern terms, a word that manages to cause much confusion is MASTHEAD. This is the publishing information found on the editorial pages of newspapers, and somewhere within magazines or other periodicals. The word comes, obviously, from the masthead of a ship; the connection between the two is simply that both show identification. Perhaps the fact that the masthead of a ship has a flag flying from it causes the common error of calling the FLAG (nameplate on the front page) of a publication the masthead. The sources that equate the two and perpetuate the confusion are doing a disservice. The distinctions between some terms are worth a struggle to preserve. (The battles continue for distinctions between *gathering* and *collating; biweekly* and *semiweekly;* and *em* and *pica.*)

Lord Northcliffe first used the name TABLOID for half-size compact newspapers, thereby calling down the wrath of the owner of the trademark *Tabloid,* designating a kind of compressed medical tablet. The trademark owner took the matter to court and got an injunction saying that the term could not be used for newspapers, but the damage had been done; Northcliffe dropped it, but others picked it up, and tabloid newspapers are here to stay.

Another kind of medicine lent its name to BROMIDE, for a cliché or trite expression. It fits quite well, for a bromide is a sedative. Mencken claims that Gelett Burgess launched *bromide* in *Burgess Unabridged* in 1914.[18]

YELLOW JOURNALISM, for sensational presentation of news, gained its name during a circulation war between two New York papers in the 1890's. *Webster's New World Dictionary's* etymology says "from the use of yellow ink, to attract readers, in printing the 'Yellow Kid,' a cartoon strip, in the *New York World* (1895)." This agrees with the *Oxford English Dictionary:* "originally U.S.: from a picture in the *New York World*, 1895, with the central figure in a yellow dress." Yet Funk & Wagnalls *Standard* says ". . . a cartoon strip, 'The Yellow Kid,' in the *New York Journal,* commencing 1896." Frank Luther Mott provides the evidence to resolve what appears to be a discrepancy in dates. He says that "The Yellow Kid," by Richard F. Outcault, was first in the *New York World* about 1895, and ". . . the color-man on the *World* had the idea of making the long, wide dress of the central 'kid' a solid and brilliant yellow." In another year, Outcault was lured over to Hearst's Sunday *Journal,* but George B. Luks took over the *World,* and "the town had two Yellow Kids every Sunday."[19]

MUCKRAKER was an epithet intended by Theodore Roosevelt to flay the sensibilities of the crusading journalists who looked only at the "muck" they were raking underfoot, as did the character in Bunyan's *Pilgrim's Progress,* and neglected to see the stars overhead. But the term became a prize of battle, for the gentlemen and ladies of the press were turning over muck at the turn of the century that had long needed turning. Roosevelt made his speech in 1906, and inadvertently provided the respected name for an era of reform touched off by conscientious journalists. They attacked the meatpacking industry, child labor, patent medicines, trusts, insurance, police corruption, and a host of social ills.[20]

STRINGER is a rather odd name for a newspaper correspondent, just a short time back more commonly called a *string correspondent*. It designates a correspondent who is paid space rates, that is, for the amount of space his copy takes up. In order to measure, the copy is pasted together in a STRING.[21]

The origin of FLACK, for press agent, seems impossible to track down. The American dictionaries have only a question mark for etymology, and the slang dictionaries give no clue. The only one to make an attempt is Mencken, who says,

Variety calls press agents *flacks,* a World War II term for antiaircraft fire. It was borrowed from the German *flak,* an abbreviation of *Fliegerabwehrkanone,* an antiaircraft cannon. Agents of extraordinary virulence are *blast artists.* They call themselves *publicists, public relations counsel* or *publicity engineers.*[22]

The connection seems tenuous, and etymologists apparently steer clear of this hypothesis. It could just as likely have come from the dialectal English *flack,* (perhaps now archaic) meaning "to flap or flutter," as given in the *Oxford English* and *Century* dictionaries.

In spite of a great deal of searching (a series of *water hauls,* according to the glossary), the origins of several intriguing terms remain a mystery. One of these is BULLDOG EDITION; none of the sources even give a date signifying when it was first used. DOCTOR BLADE presents another puzzle. It is very old; the *Oxford English Dictionary* has a 1796 citation for ". . . steel doctors for printers." ("Doctor" alone without the "blade.") It was, and perhaps is, applied to various other blade-like devices used with machinery.

JEFF has only an 1888 citation in the *Oxford English Dictionary* with no etymology. It is apparently an Americanism, as the *Dictionary of American English* has an 1837 citation, along with the same one given in the OED.

FUDGE BOX is a rather mixed-up term. The *Oxford English Dictionary* gives an archaic sense "to patch or contrive," (for FUDGE), which *Century* enlarges upon: "In printing, to make use of improper materials or methods to produce a needed result with greater speed." This verb sense is followed by the noun:

2. in newspaper parlance, matter of supposed importance, as the latest sporting news or sensational stuff, which comes to hand too late to find a place on the plates before going to press and is inserted in a special place by cutting the plates. See *fudge-box*. 3. in printing, an unworkmanlike practice.

The sense following describes homemade candy, and ends with a note, "The name alludes to the hasty amateur manufacture," which would make it appear that *Century* assumes the name of the candy came from the printing term.[23] The printing sense is not in some other sources, as those for slang or printing terms. FUDGE BOX, in Merriam-Webster's *Third Edition* is, for its first sense, "the metal container in a newspaper printing press for holding fudge matter."

The first citation for LOBSTER TRICK in the *Dictionary of Americanisms* came from the *New York Telegram* in 1930, and Weingarten's *American Dictionary of Slang's* first date is 1933. One guess as to its origin was suggested by an *Editor & Publisher* contributor: "Lobster trick staffers go to work long before sunup at an hour when late lobster supper parties are popularly supposed to disperse and only an owl could see without artificial light."[24] This explanation seems a bit tentative.

The origin of BRISTOL BOARD is quite prosaic; it was named for the city of Bristol, England. FREE-LANCER is more dashing and romantic, for the term was originally applies to medieval mercenary soldiers. If the pen is mightier than the sword, the appellation is still apropos.

Other terms that looked as though they might be interesting, but turned into nothing, were PHAT, only a variant of *fat*, and QUOIN, only a variant of *coin*. However, the latter is ultimately from the Latin *cuneus*, a wedge, so QUOIN is closer to the original meaning than is *coin*. Another word that remains rather perplexing is NEMO, for a broadcast that originates away from the studio. Most sources feel that it is a reshuffling of the word *remote*, with perhaps some influence from *nemo*, Latin for no one. But this may be conjecture; no one seems to know who coined it, nor gives a date to indicate when it was first used.

The natural place to end a discussion of the origin of journalism terms is THIRTY, or often -30-, both because of its meaning—the end of a story—and because it is the most disputed of all. Some of the more timid compilers of terms, or those with limited space, enter it simply as "a symbol used to denote the end of a story" and let it go at that. But those who like to live dangerously venture an opinion. One theory is that it was a telegrapher's XXX, and this is given by Wentworth and Flexner's *Dictionary of American Slang*, and Arnold. The latter's entry is *30-dash*, as is *Random House Dictionary's*—which is not surprising, seeing that Arnold did the printing and bookbinding terms for Random House.

Mitford Mathews, dean of American lexicographers, indulges in a fancy in *American Speech* to pass on a ludicrous story:

. . . Gordon B. Wheeler, of Hinsdale, Illinois, . . . writes me that until he has received positive proof to the contrary, he is going to maintain that whoever first used *thirty* as printers and telegraphers do to mean "the end," might well have derived his inspiration from John Foxe's work on martyrs. Mr. Wheeler finds in this work the detailed account of the torture and death of a Bohemian minister during the reign of Ferdinand II (1619–37). The horrible things done to this poor wretch are listed in order and numbered. They total thirty. The last torture consisted of twisting a cord about the minister's head until death followed. Mr. Wheeler concludes his presentation of this enumeration of tortures with "30 was the end, wasn't it?"[25]

Jahn's entry is *thirty-rule,* which seems to rather go with Arnold's *30-dash.* Jahn defines it like this: "A rule or dash line, of arbitrary length, used in newspaper offices at the end of an article, when all the takes have been set. The final or finish-rule."[26]

To rather echo this, or bolster it, is a note from the *Webster's New World Dictionary* files written by a former editor: "probably so called from a line of 30 ems across the width of a column between articles."[27]

Mencken contents himself by footnoting to several sources where one could look it up. Mentioned first is the Chicago *Tribune.*

The Chicago *Tribune* for January 13, 1940, in a column called "A LINE O' TYPE OR TWO" by Charles Collins, presented this (brackets are Collins') :

ORIGIN OF THIRTY

"Thirty" originated among telegraph operators, who have quite a vocabulary of numbers for technical use. For example: 1 means "wait a minute"; . . . 7, "go ahead"; . . . 13, "what's the matter?"; . . . 30, "end of item"; 73, "kindest regards." Most of these symbols appear to have been invented by Walter P. Phillips, whose code has been in use for more than fifty years. But neither 30 nor 73, the commonest, appear in his original codebook. They may easily be almost a hundred years old. [The first use of telegraphy dates back 96 years.]

The origin of 30 is a mystery. We have interviewed five telegraph operators without getting a clew to it. There has been a great deal of theorizing behind this symbol, which often appears on floral pieces at funerals of the newspaper crafts, and we will give seven explanations, plausible, implausible, and incredible, in Monday's column.

True to his word, on January 15 came (again, bracketed comments are Collins') :

SEVEN THEORIES ABOUT THIRTY

1. When newspaper articles were written by hand and set in type by hand, a period was indicated in the manuscript by an "x," the end of a paragraph by "xx," and the end of the item by "xxx," which looks like the Roman numerals for 30.

2. It came out of India via England. In the Bengali language 80 means "Farewell," or "I quit." [*But why?*] An English officer in Calcutta used 80 at the end of a letter to the British East India company, written in 1758. The company published the letter, but a typographical error turned the 80 into 30. [*To this theory we say, in the Bengali language, "Tosh."*]

3. Typesetting machines that cast their type in slug form used to set a maximum length of line known to printers as 30 pica ems, and 30 meant the end of the line. [*Oldtime printers reject this explanation and state that the symbol antedates slug-casting machines by many years.*]

4. During a disaster [not mentioned], information was wired to the newspapers by a telegrapher whose number was 30. He remained at his key until he was drowned, or burned, or blown up, or something. [*This is the inevitable sentimental explanation; we reject it.*]

5. A telegrapher in the wild west, before newspapers had wires into their offices, used to write dispatches in longhand and send them by messenger. His office closed at 3, and at the bottom of his last sheet he always wrote 3 o'clock, which became corrupted into 3 o'c, 3 o, and 30. [*We doubt it.*]

6. When the Associated Press was established, each member was entitled to 30 telegrams every 24 hours. The last message was marked 30.

7. Sparta appointed 30 magistrates to rule over Athens at the close of the Peloponnesian war. They were called the Thirty Tyrants. There was great rejoicing when they were overthrown. [*Nobody will swallow this one.*]

[*Research by Charles W. Harper of the Utica, New York Press; first published in Editor and Publisher, 1932*].

Apparently as soon as this column appeared in the *Tribune*, Mr. Collins received the "true story," as the following day, January 16, his column contained this tidbit:

APPROVED THEORY FOR ORIGIN OF THIRTY

The earliest organization which presented any semblance to a press association came into being in Washington in the 1870s. It specialized in news of congress, the administration, and the Supreme Court.

A few news writers got together and peddled their wares to a few New York, Boston, Albany, and Chicago papers in the beginning, and these papers were connected directly with Washington by means of Western Union wires, for which they paid regular press rate tolls. It was not until some years later there was an incorporated press association which leased wire service.

Receiving operators copied the reports with a stylus, making from 4 to 13 carbon copies. Their wire form required the separating of each item or story with the letter X below the article and in the center of the last sheet. At the end of the report—when there was no more matter to

be transmitted, about 3:30 in the morning—the form was
to place triple X after the last item, so that when it reached
the telegraph editor's desk he would know that was all for
the night. Since XXX represents the Roman numerals for
30, the figure 30 came into general use with the introduction of the typewriter in press work in the early '90s.

E.E.B.

[This information comes from E. E. Bruckner, assistant
traffic manager of the Western Union Telegraph company
in Chicago. He got it from Walter P. Phillips, compiler of
the Phillips code book. He worked with Phillips on a revi-
sion of the code book in 1914.]

Arthur Robb, in the department, "Shop Talk at Thirty,"
in *Editor & Publisher*, May, 1940, repeated the theories
given in the Chicago *Tribune*.[28]

American Notes and Queries had a series of letters and
discussions about THIRTY in the July and August issues
of 1941 and January of 1942. The theories discussed were
the same as those in the Chicago *Tribune*, and *Editor &
Publisher*, for the most part. Comments differing from, or
taking exception to, the theories given in those sources
were these:

There is another story to the effect that long, long ago a
printer dropped dead in the printing office and that he
happened to have in his hand at the time a type bar with
the figure "30" on it.

It is also said that old-time operators sending news telegrams to newspapers used "30" at the end of news telegrams to indicate that the story not only was ended but
that it came collect. . . . I can't find . . . that newspapers
ever were restricted to an even thirty telegrams.

I don't think there is much basis . . . for the belief that
"30" came from "3 o'clock" to indicate the time that telegraph offices closed each morning. It's my understanding

that the first telegraph offices closed much earlier than 3:00 a.m.

Oliver Gramling[29]

Another traditional speculation is passed along by Roland Wolseley:

The common explanation of 30 I have always heard is that an Irish telegraph operator by the name of Thurty decided to sign off with 30 instead of spelling out his name in Morse code.[30]

This explanation is also given in a Cleveland *Plain Dealer* article datelined Hollywood, California, in 1959. The article also offers two more possible origins of the term. A compositor in Chicago said that in the pre-typewriter era of journalism when copy was written in longhand, "a numerical symbol was used to indicate clearly the end of their stories." But, says the feature, "why was the symbol 30 and not 40 or 50?" It attributes another story to a headline writer of a Philadelphia paper, who claimed that "it stemmed from the fact that 30 words was just the right fit in a stick of type" in the days when newspaper body type was set by hand.[31] One must assume he meant "characters" rather than "words," but the wider columns of newspapers in bygone days makes this story a bit unlikely.

Thus we have a dozen or more stories to explain the origin of the use of 30. The mystery remains.

And this, perhaps, is a good place to write

— 30 —

II. A Glossary of Print-communications Terms

ACETATE   a transparent plastic substance, used as a film base, for coatings on phonograph records, or in sheets. The sheets may hold inked type impressions, to be used as positives in photomechanical reproduction (*acetate proofs*), or as overlays on artwork for mechanical color separation, with each of two or more sheets showing the portion to be printed a specified color.

ACTINIC RAYS   short-wave light rays, as violet or ultraviolet, that produce chemical changes in photography.

AD ALLEY   the section of the composing room where ads are made up: sometimes called *ad side* or *ad-side*.

ADD   new copy to be added to a story already written. The second page of a story sent to a newspaper composing room, or the second section of a story filed with a wire news service is slugged "add 1," the next "add 2," etc.

ADDENDUM   material added at the end of a book, necessary to its completeness, shorter than a supplement. It may be material inadvertently omitted, or corrections (see ERRATA), or it could be material that became available after the main body of the book was set into type: distinguished from APPENDIX.

ADMAN   1. a man who works in advertising, especially one who writes advertising copy. 2. a compositor who sets advertising matter.

---

*Entries followed by a star are discussed in Chapter I, section entitled "Origins of Some Journalism Terms."

ADVANCE (COPY), ADVANCER   release copy, held for publication until a release date.

AFGHANISTANISM   a newspaper's avoidance of controversial local issues and causes by focusing attention on faraway events.

AGATE   1. a small size type, approximately 5½ point.[1] 2. a hand tool with an agate (stone) head, used by gilders to burnish gold or silver edges on books.

AGATE LINE   a unit of measurement for classified advertising in newspapers and magazines, approximately $\frac{1}{14}$ inch deep and one column wide; thus there are 14 lines to the column inch.[2]

AGENCE FRANCE PRESS   the wire news service of France.[3]

AGONY COLUMN   the classified column for personal messages, as for those trying to contact missing relatives, etc.

AIRBRUSH   a fine sprayer, operated by compressed air, used in retouching photographs, spraying pigment on artwork, or laying a protective or finishing coat on a surface, as of paper.

ALBUMEN PLATE   a printing plate coated with egg albumen and prepared by photomechanical methods: the most common kind used for offset lithography, usually for short runs (less than 50,000).

ALDINE   designating a book, edition, or style of type from the press of Aldus Manutius of Venice in the sixteenth century.

ALIBI COPY   duplicate copy filed in the morgue.

ALIGN   to bring into a stright line, as type along a common baseline, or to straighten margins, columns of figures, etc. Also spelled *aline*. When letters are in a straight line, they are in *alignment* (*alinement*).

ALIVE (or LIVE)   1. designating type after it has been set, at any time until it is ready for distribution. 2. designating a microphone, sound system, etc. that is turned on and in operation.

ALLEGE   to state or assert, especially, to declare without proof. A "weasel word" used frequently by journalists to establish a defense against libel.[4]

ALLEY   an aisle in a printshop or composing room between type cabinets or typesetting machines.

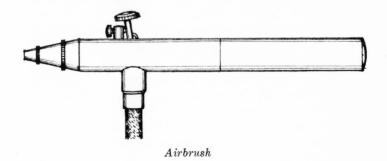

Airbrush

ALL UP   1. designating copy that has been all set into type.   2. indicating that all copy sent to a compositor has been set.

ALPHA DELTA SIGMA   advertising fraternity, founded in 1913.

ALPHA EPSILON RHO   broadcasting fraternity, founded in 1943.

ALPHA PHI GAMMA   journalism fraternity, founded in 1919.

ALTERATION   a change in copy by the author after it has been set in type: also *author's alteration, author's correction,* or *AA.* An expensive process, charged to the publisher, who sometimes charges AA's against the author's royalties, especially if considered unreasonable. Distinguished from corrections that occur because of a printer's error (PE).

AMERICAN NEWSPAPER GUILD   a labor union of newspaper, magazine, and wire service employees, affiliated with the AFL/CIO.

AMIDOL   a photographic developer.

AMPERSAND   a symbol (&) used for the word "and": sometimes called the *short and.* It was first formed by combining the letters of the Latin word for "and," *et,* and in some forms these two letters are clearly distinguishable. It is often written *&c* or *&c.* for *et cetera.*

ANAGLYPH   a three-dimensional illustration or motion picture.

ANATOLIE news service in Turkey.

ANGLE 1. the point of view from which something is written [this is from the woman's *angle*]: *slant* has connotations of being used for an expression of bias that *angle* does not have. 2. to write something from a certain point of view.

ANGSTROM (UNIT) a unit of measurement of the wavelength of light: one 100 millionth of a centimeter.

ANIMATED CARTOON 1. a film, usually short, consisting of photographic frames of drawn pictures, each slightly changed from the last, which, run off in proper succession, give the impression of moving characters. 2. a similar effect achieved by successive patterns in lights, used in advertising displays. 3. a similar effect achieved by revolving or rearranging billboard panels.

ANTIMONY one of the ingredients of type metal; antimony gives hardness to the alloy.

ANTIQUE 1. a bulky book paper with a somewhat rough finish. 2. a style of type with a heavy face. 3. see BLIND (stamping).

APPENDIX material added at the end of a book, not properly part of the text, but planned as a part of the book: distinguished from ADDENDUM or SUPPLEMENT.

AQUATINT 1. an etching process in which successive portions of a rosin-coated plate are stopped out with acid resist between bites of acid: see STOP OUT. 2. an etching produced by this process, resembling a wash drawing or water color.

AQUATONE   1. a printing method in which a zinc plate is coated with gelatin, hardened and sensitized to print fine-screen halftones, type, line cuts, etc.   2. a print produced by this method.

ARTWORK   1. a piece of work in the graphic arts, creatively produced.   2. the process of creating this.   3. a mechanical or paste-up, composed of proofs of type or illustrations, lettering, line drawings, etc.   4. any of the elements used in a mechanical, especially those done by hand.

ASCENDERS   1. the lines or loops of type that extend above the x-height of the letters.   2. the letters themselves, as lower case b, d, h, etc.

ASSOCIATED PRESS   a cooperative wire news service, owned by its member newspapers, radio and television stations. Members put their local major news stories on the wire for fellow members to use as desired, although the main daily report of national and international news, along with features, news analyses, photographs, etc., is issued by the staff in offices situated throughout the country and overseas. AP started in 1848 and has over 8,000 members.[5]

ASTERISK   a reference mark (*).

ASTONISHER   1. an exclamation point.   2. a large, bold headline; screamer.

AUDIO   the sound part of a television broadcast or film.

AUDIOVISUAL   having to do with media or devices that make use of both sight and sound, as supplements to textbooks in teaching.

AUDIT BUREAU OF CIRCULATIONS   an organization that issues periodic audited reports stating the circulation of publications, as magazines and newspapers, which must have 70% or more paid circulation to be members.[6] It was formed in 1914 by a merger of the Advertising Audit Association and the Bureau of Verified Circulations.

AUTHOR'S ALTERATION (or CORRECTION) see AL-TERATION.

AX-GRINDER   1. a person, as a publicist, who supplies news to a paper or wire news service in order to gain publicity, usually for a client.   2. an editorial written carefully so that it appears to be objective, but that is actually slanted.

AYER'S DIRECTORY   a directory issued periodically, and listing pertinent, up-to-date data about newspapers and magazines, as address, editor, publisher, circulation, etc.

BACKBONE   1. the bound edge of a book, connecting front and back covers: also called *backstrip, shelfback, spine, back*.   2. a wire between wire news service bureaus for messages not seen by the clients: used for requests for, or for sending, specific information or stories[7]: also called *overhead* or shortened to *bone:* distinguished from *news wire,* which is for general use.

BACK MATTER   material at the end of a book, following the main body: it may include appendix, index, bibliography, notes, addendum, errata, glossary, supplement, etc.: sometimes written *backmatter,* or called *end matter* or *reference matter.*

BACK UP   to print the reverse side of a sheet already printed on one side; perfect.

BAKED   describing type that is caked or sticks together and is hard to separate for distribution.

BANK   1. one of the divisions of two or more lines of a headline, especially a lower one; deck.   2. a table or bench, often slant-topped, on which type in galleys is kept or worked on.   3. the personnel of a department or section of a newspaper staff [the rewrite *bank*].

BANNER   the front page headline in large type that extends the width of the page: also *banner head.*

BARKER   a reverse kicker: see KICKER.

BASELINE   the horizontal bottom line along which letters are aligned.

BASIS (WEIGHT)   the weight in pounds of 500 (sometimes 1,000) sheets of paper of a certain size: also called *basic weight, substance.*[8]

BASTARD   1. designating type of an irregular size, not made to point standard: see POINT SYSTEM.   2. designating type cast on a body size inappropriate to its face size.   3. designating a page bearing only the name of the book, preceding the title page; half title.

BATTER   broken or flattened type, or a damaged area of a printing plate. Type is sometimes battered (*disfigured*) deliberately if an objectionable word or phrase is discovered after the form is on the press.

BEARD   the bevel of a piece of type, or, often, the bevel and shoulder together. See illustration for TYPE.

BEARER   a type-high rule, often 2 picas wide, set around the sides of a type form, or metal left around a photo-engraving, to help distribute the pressure of molding and protect the printing surfaces; dead metal.

BEAT   1. to get ahead of rival publications in publishing a timely news story; scoop.   2. such a news story; scoop; exclusive.   3. a regular area for newsgathering assigned to a reporter.

BENDAY or BEN DAY PROCESS   shading, as a pattern of dots, dashed lines, or other textures, used in photo-engraving as the background or fill-in for patterns on artwork.[9] Benday is added to the plates as they are being etched. Cf. ZIP-A-TONE, CRAFTINT.

BEVEL   1. the slanted edge of a piece of type: see NECK.   2. the edge of a halftone plate, about ⅛″, used as a flange so that the plate can be tacked on a wood base.   3. the sloping edge of a stereotype or electrotype plate, by which the plate is fastened to the base.   4. a slug cast with a beveled edge for placing around cuts.   5. to slant the edges of a book board for the cover by sanding, etc.

BIBLE PAPER   a strong, thin paper that is opaque, used for printing Bibles, dictionaries, etc.

BIMONTHLY   a publication that appears once every two months: distinguished from SEMIMONTHLY.

BITE   1. to etch with acid.   2. the etching action of acid, or an instance of this.

BIWEEKLY   a publication that appears once every two weeks: distinguished from SEMIWEEKLY.

BLACKITE   black and white: said of magazine illustrations.

BLACK LETTER   class of heavy-faced type based on hand lettering (German) as done in the days before movable type. Often called *text* or *Old English*.

BLACK LIGHT   infrared or ultraviolet rays, used for photography in the dark, or for fluorescent lighting effects.

BLACKSMITH   an inferior reporter; one who merely "pounds out" news stories.

BLANKET   in offset, the rubber covering of the roller that offsets the image onto the paper.

BLANKET HEAD   a headline that extends across all the columns having to do with a particular story.

BLEED   to run off the edge of a page, with the excess trimmed off: said of an illustration, usually in a magazine. Originally said of pages with margins trimmed so close that the printing was cut, and still sometimes used in this sense.

BLIND said of a design that is impressed or embossed on paper, a book cover, etc., without using ink or gold leaf: also called *blank* or *antique stamping* or *tooling*.

BLIND LEAD a lead of a news story that does not identify the subject immediately. Example: "A woman in black sat in a courtroom in Atlanta today." The second paragraph then identifies the woman by name, and proceeds to fill in the five W's.

BLOCK British term for CUT (senses 1 and 2).

BLOCK LETTER a printed or hand-printed letter that is simple in form and without serifs: SANS SERIF type is sometimes called block letter.

BLOW UP to enlarge a photograph. BLOW-UP the photograph thus enlarged.

BLUE-PENCIL to edit.

BLUEPRINT a fast contact print from an offset negative or flat, used as a proof: also called *blueline* or *blue*.

BLURB★ an overly enthusiastic advertisement or publicity release: originally used to describe publishers' statements on book jackets.

BODY 1. the whole of a piece of type except for the printing surface; shank. See illustration for TYPE. 2. the dimension of a type from front to back, as a 6-point face on an 8-point body.[10] 3. type commonly used for straight matter, as the text of a book, newspaper, etc., as distinguished from that used for headings, display, footnotes, etc.: in full, *body type*. 4. the main text of a book, following the FRONT MATTER, and before the BACK MATTER.

BOGUS   1. fillers or timeless features printed in an early edition, to be replaced by news in a later edition. 2. matter set by union requirements that has been previously stereotyped.

BOIL DOWN   to make a news story more concise by cutting out portions; reduce wordage.

BOILERPLATE   1. stereotype plates, often . of syndicated material, furnished to a newspaper ready to be mounted.   2. the literary content of such plates: a derogatory term.

BOND   a fine, strong paper with high rag content, used for stationery, etc.

BONE   see BACKBONE (sense 2).

BOOK   1. a number of printed pages or signatures bound together, and differentiated from a pamphlet, magazine, etc. by size and form.   2. in the parlance of magazinists, a magazine.

BOTTLED   an old term used to describe type that is badly worn and cannot stand upon its feet.

BOURGEOIS★   a size of type, approximately 9 point.

BOURGES   a trademark for colored acetate sheets, keyed to standard printing inks, for use as overlays on artwork and layouts.

BOX   1. a printed rectangle or square made with type rules for enclosing type matter.   2. the copy so enclosed. Legibility studies indicate a box set around news sometimes acts as a barrier affecting eye movement. In an effort to overcome this, yet still use boxes for special effects, modern layout men often specify boxes that are open on the sides (thus not really boxes at all) so that the eye may easily "move in" to the copy. They may also use boxes made of a border that will print as gray rather than black.

BOXED HEADLINES   headlines enclosed, usually on the top and sides, with rules.

L **BRACKETED SERIF (CASLON)**

BRACKETED SERIF   a serif that curves as it connects with a main stroke of a letter.

BRAYER★   roller used to apply ink by hand for pulling proofs, or to apply ink or paint in artwork.

BREAK   1. the point at which a story is broken off to be continued on another page.   2. the portion of a story continued on another page or column; jump: sometimes also called *breakover* or *runover*.   3. to occur: said of news when it is available for publication.   4. station identification on radio or TV.

BREAKLINE   1. the last line of a paragraph.   2. the last line of a column or page of a story that is continued on another page.

BREAK-OFF RULE   a rule set clear across one or more columns to indicate that the copy above and below are not related.

BREAK-OF-THE-BOOK   the allocation of space in a magazine.

BREVIER★   a size of type, approximately 8 point.

BRILLIANT★   a size of type, varying between 3½ and 4 point: it is 3½ point in England, where it is also called *half-minion:* see TYPE SIZES.

BRISTOL BOARD★   a thin, smooth-surfaced cardboard used for artwork, especially line drawing, hand lettering, etc.

BRITE or BRIGHT   a short, human-interest feature of one or two paragraphs; it "brightens up" the newspaper.

BROADSIDE   1. a large sheet printed on one side only, usually with advertising or promotional matter, or an official announcement: sometimes called *broadsheet.* 2. a large, specially-folded advertising sheet, printed on one or both sides.[11]

BROCHURE   a booklet or pamphlet, usually designed with restraint and with some elegance, and with a special cover.

BROMIDE★   a cliché; stereotyped expression.

BUG   1. any type ornament; dingbat.   2. a telegrapher's key, especially one that is high-speed, with automatic repeating operation for dots and dashes.

BULK   1. the relative thickness of paper.   2. the thickness of a book from front to back, exclusive of the cover.

BULLDOG EDITION★   the early edition of a newspaper.

BULLET   any of several sizes of heavy periods, set at the beginning of succeeding lines of type to draw attention to specific major points being made in the text.

BULLETIN   1. a brief lead of last-minute information, often printed at the head of the story to which it is related.   2. a wire service news message of more than ordinary importance.   3. a timely or important news flash presented on radio or TV.   4. a regular publication of an organization, or a college catalog, brochure, etc.

BULLPUP EDITION   the first mail edition of a Sunday newspaper.

BUMPING HEADS   very black headlines of the same size, side by side; tombstones.

BUN   short for BULLETIN.

BURIN   an engraver's pointed cutting tool, usually steel.

BURN IN   in photography, to give more definition to certain portions of a print during the printing process, by exposing to more light, applying extra developer, rubbing the print, etc.: opposed to DODGE.

BURNISH   to shine, polish, or rub metal, especially (a) to rub down some of the halftone dots on a plate in order to make the dots larger; the plate will then print darker in that section. (b) to polish off some of the roughened areas on a mezzotint plate. (c) to rub gold leaf into place on book edges with an agate burnisher.

BURR   rough edges of metal, raised in routing, graving, etc.

BURY A STORY   to place a story on an inside page.

BUSINESS PUBLICATION AUDIT OF CIRCULATION an organization that issues periodic audited reports stating the circulation of publications, as magazines and newspapers which have less than 70% paid circulation. It was founded in 1931 and was called Controlled Circulation Audit until 1954.

BUTT   1. to place two linotype slugs side by side to make a longer line: a linecaster will ordinarily set a line of 30 picas maximum length.   2. to place two printing plates together so that the shoulders are on the sides that do not adjoin.

BYLINE name of the journalist who wrote a story, printed just below the heading, or, occasionally, at the end of the story.[12]

CALENDERED   designating paper that has been passed between polished steel *calender rolls,* giving it a smooth surface: see SUPER.

CALIFORNIA JOB CASE a shallow tray with 89 compartments in which type characters for a given font are kept, including upper and lower case letters, figures, special characters, spacing, etc.

		5-EM	4-EM	'	k		1	2	3	4	5	6	7	8	$	£					
ffi	fl																				
j	b	c	d	e		i	s	f	g	ff	9	A	B	C	D	E	F	G
?										fi	0							
!	l	m	n	h	o	y	p	w	,	EN QUADS	EM QUADS	H	I	K	L	M	N	O
z																		
x	v	u	t	3-EM SPACES	a	r	;	:	2-EM AND 3-EM QUADS	P	Q	R	S	T	V	W
q							.	-		X	Y	Z	J	U	&	ffl

California job case

CALLIGRAPHY fine handwriting, developed as an art and used for lettering in book design, advertising, and other artwork.

CANNED COPY 1. same as HANDOUT. 2. copy from news agencies, feature syndicates, etc., sometimes stereotyped.

CANON★ a very large size type, 44 or 48 point: when 48 point, also called *four-line pica:* see TYPE SIZES.

CAPTION 1. a heading or title over a picture: distinguished from CUTLINE. 2. loosely, any explanatory matter with an illustration, as a cutline: considered by many to be an inaccurate usage. 3. a heading for a chapter, article, or table.

CARBON TISSUE a light-sensitized paper with a gelatin coating, used in the production of printing plates for gravure, photogravure, and rotogravure printing. When the photographic film positive is exposed through the carbon tissue, exposure to the light hardens the gelatin most in the lightest areas, and to varying degrees elsewhere. After exposure, the tissue is applied to the plate, and the soluble gelatin is washed away, leaving an image in hardened gelatin of varying thicknesses.

CARET★ a mark (∧) indicating where a letter, word, etc. is to be inserted.

CASE a shallow tray or drawer with compartments in which type is kept: in a pair of *news cases,* the *upper case* is for capital letters, small capitals, special characters, etc., and the *lower case* for small letters, figures, etc.[13] The most commonly used case today is the CALIFORNIA JOB CASE, which see.

CASING-IN the final step in binding a book; putting the cover on: see FORWARDING.

CASTER (PLATE) an electrotype plate used as a master for casting plates: distinguished from WORKER.

CAST-OFF an estimate of the amount of space a piece of copy or a manuscript will occupy when set in a given typeface. The process of estimating is called *casting off,* or COPYFITTING.

CATCHLINE see SLUG (sense 3).

CATCHWORD word at the top of a reference book column: the left one gives the first word on the page; the right gives the word last in alphabetical order on the page: see also SLUG.

CENTER SPREAD see DOUBLE SPREAD.

CHAPEL★ an association of union members in a printshop.

CHASE a metal frame in which a form of printing elements is locked up for printing or for the preparation of duplicate printing plates.

CHINESE WHITE   an opaque enamel-like pigment used for patching up errors in lettering, or for opaquing out backgrounds in photography: also called *zinc white*.

CHROMA   the degree of intensity of a color.

CIRCULARS   advertisements or promotional pieces produced in quantity and passed out by hand, sent by direct mail, etc.

CIRCULATION   the average number of copies of a publication sold or distributed in a given period: see also READERSHIP.

CIRCUS MAKEUP   on a newspaper page, the use of a number of styles and sizes of type in headlines, with no apparent system or design.

CITY EDITOR   the editor in a newspaper office in charge of local news: his domain is the *city room*.

CLAMSHELL   platen press: also *clapper*.

CLASSIFIED   designating newspaper or magazine advertisements that are grouped into categories, as real estate, help wanted, automotive, etc., and printed in blocks, usually in agate type: also called *want-ads*. See note at AGATE.

CLEAN   indicating copy that requires few changes or little copy editing, or proof that needs few corrections.

CLICHÉ   an overused, trite expression; bromide.[14]

CLICKER   1. a die-cutting machine: also *clicking ma-_ chine*.   2. *British*   a compositor foreman or supervisor.

CLOSE   to finish preparations for printing a magazine; put to bed.

CLOSING DATE   the day on which all copy must be submitted in order to appear in a magazine or other publication: generally, the same as DEADLINE, though the latter may apply to an hour as well as a day.

CLOZE PROCEDURE   a readability test, developed by Dr. Wilson L. Taylor, that measures the relative ease of reading a piece of copy by deleting evenly spaced words, replacing them with blank spaces, and seeing how many words the members of a chosen group can fill in.

CLUMP   British term for SLUG (sense 2).

COCKLED   designating the condition of paper or books that are wrinkled, warped, curled, buckled, etc. from high humidity or temperature. Also, a pebbled effect deliberately achieved on some kinds of bond paper.

COLD DOPE   statistics.

COLD TYPE   any printing method, usually photographic, that does not use molten metal: opposed to HOT TYPE.

COLLAGE   artwork produced by pasting up a variety of clippings, pictures, bits of string, wood, etc., sometimes but not always related by subject matter, color, tone, etc. Distinguished from MONTAGE.

COLLATING   1. the examination of a book, booklet, etc. after gathering, to see that signatures, sheets, plates, maps, etc. are in the proper order. *Collating marks* are often printed on the sheets that form the outside of a signature, in a successive pattern that may be checked easily. Distinguished from GATHERING.   2. loosely, same as GATHERING: widely used, but considered by some to be an inaccurate usage.   3. the process of comparing prints of fine or rare books, letter for letter, with attention to minute details of typography.   4. by a device on a duplicator (*collator*), the separating of successively printed pages into a series of usually slanted receptacles so that each receptacle holds a completed set of sheets in proper order.

COLLOTYPE★   lithographic printing from an image prepared by a photomechanical process on a film of hardened gelatin; photogelatin; used for high quality continuous-tone prints.[15]

*Cornell
University Press*

*Kent State
University Press*

*Syracuse
University Press*

Colophons

COLOPHON   1. a publisher's emblem, printed on the title page and spine of a book.   2. an inscription at the end of a book, giving information about its production, as the printer's name, kind of type used, etc.

COLOR SEPARATION   the breaking down of full-color copy into primary colors, as: (a) a set of drawings on acetate sheets, one of each of the colors to be printed: each is prepared as an overlay on the key or original drawing, and is used in making one of the printing plates: sometimes called *mechanical separation.* (b) a set of negatives, each exposed through the proper filter to take out all but the color wanted.[16]

COLUMBIAN★   1. a large size type, approximately 16 point: in England, called *two-line brevier:* see also ENGLISH.   2. the first printing press invented in America.[17]

COMBINATION PLATE   a photoengraving printing plate that carries both halftone and line work.

COMMA CHASER   a copy editor.

COMPOSING STICK   a metal receptacle into which single types are assembled in hand composition.

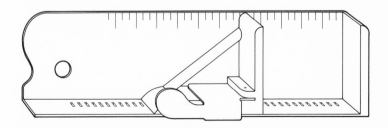

Composing Stick

COMPOSITOR   a person whose work is *composition,* the setting of type and assembling this with engravings or other printing elements into pages ready for the press; typesetter.

COMPREHENSIVE   a completed layout of correct size and with artwork and type in proper relative position, and with details indicated: used especially of an advertisement, and often shorted to *comp.*

CONDENSED   designating a typeface that is narrower than the standard type of the same design, as "Spartan Medium Condensed." Sometimes called *compressed* by the British. Opposed to EXPANDED.

CONTACT PRINT   a photographic print made by direct contact of the negative with the printing paper, film, plate, etc., and thus the same size.

CONTINUOUS TONE   said of a photographic image, or picture, in which the density varies continuously from dark to light shades. This is the kind of image used for a HALFTONE.

CONTRASTY   designating a drawing, photograph, etc., that has good contrast, thus will reproduce well.

CONTROLLED CIRCULATION   designating a magazine or newspaper that is sent free to members of a specific business, profession, trade, etc., or residents of a given geographic area. These publications are usually financed by advertising.

COPY   1. any or all written material.   2. generally, any material to be printed or reproduced, as a manuscript, illustrations, advertising, etc.   3. a single magazine, newspaper, book, etc.

COPY EDITOR   1. a publishing house editor who reviews a manuscript for style, grammar, etc. and marks it for the printer.   2. a newspaper employee who does this for news copy: often called *copyreader*.   3. a newspaper editor in charge of copyreaders: see also SLOT.

COPYFITTING   the process of figuring how much space the type set from a given amount of copy will occupy, or fitting a given amount of copy into an allotted space by the use of different sizes or designs of type.

COPYHOLDER   a person who reads copy aloud to a proofreader, to be compared with proof.

COPYREADER   a person who edits copy; copy editor.

COPYRIGHT   the legal right to exclusive ownership of original writing or artwork, obtained by sending two copies of the published material with application forms and a fee to Washington. The term of copyright is 28 years, and may be renewed once; after 56 years, the work is in public domain. Titles may not be copyrighted.[18]

CORRESPONDENT   a reporter who sends his copy, pictures, film, etc. from a distance, by wire, mail, radio, telephone, etc.

CORRIGENDA   see ERRATA.

CORX an instruction to the printer to correct copy: sometimes *CX*.

COUNTER see SHOULDER.

COVER 1. to report news about, or take news pictures of, an event, etc. 2. a heavy paper used for covering booklets, paperback books, etc. 3. the outside sheets of a magazine,[19] and the advertising space thereon: the inside front cover is called the *second cover;* inside back, *third cover;* outside back, *fourth cover.* Space on these is sold at a premium.

CRAFTINT a trademark for plastic sheets that carry a variety of regular patterns, applied by the artist to fill in areas in artwork to be used for line cuts: compare BENDAY.

CREDIT LINE the name of the photographer, illustrator, or owner of an illustration, printed in small type just below it.

CROP to cut down the size of a photograph, usually to specific proportions: it may be done by actual trimming with a scissors, or by marking the margins with grease pencil to indicate to the photographer what area he should copy.

CROSSBAR 1. a horizontal element between the upright strokes on some letters, as A or H. 2. an attachment on some printing presses for turning or guiding paper. 3. a bar stretching across a large chase that strengthens it and helps facilitate locking up type.

CUB a beginning reporter.

CURSIVE   a typeface designed to resemble handwriting, but with the letters not connected to one another, as they are in SCRIPT.

CUT   1. originally, a woodcut; illustration engraved on a wood block.   2. now, a photoengraving, electrotype, etc.   3. to shorten copy by rewriting or by deleting ending paragraphs, etc.

CUTLINE   explanatory matter under an illustration; legend.

CUTOFF RULE   a rule used to separate advertisements, etc.; any horizontal rule.

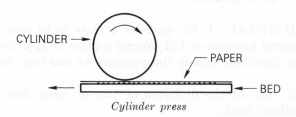

Cylinder press

CYLINDER PRESS   a printing press with a flat bed, often reciprocating, for the type form, and a cylinder which carries the paper and impresses it against the type.

DAGGER   a reference mark (†).

DANCE   type that falls out of the form as it is lifted is said to dance.

DANDY ROLL★   a wire cylinder that impresses the watermark in paper: sometimes called *dandy roller*.

DATELINE   the line at the beginning of a news story telling the point of origin of the story, and, formerly, the date. The date is seldom included in our age of rapid communication, as it can be assumed the news was dispatched on the same day the paper was issued: see also FOLIO (sense 7).

DAY SIDE   1. designating the staff of a newspaper or wire news service that works during the day.   2. the shift worked.

DEADLINE   the time at which copy must be submitted in order to be printed.

DEAD METAL   1. the parts of a plate to be routed off. 2. metal inserted or left around a plate or type form to help distribute evenly the pressure of molding; bearer.

DECK   one of the divisions of two or more lines of a headline; bank.

DECK HEAD   see DROPHEAD.

DECKLE EDGE   a feather edge on paper, originally on untrimmed handmade paper: the *deckle* was the papermaker's frame. This edge is now produced by cutting paper with a sawlike device rather than trimming with a sharp knife.

DEEP ETCH   a process in offset lithography by which the image is recessed slightly below the surface, for long runs.

DELE or DELETE   take out; remove: a proofreader's or copy editor's word: sometimes *del*. Most often signified by the symbol ☙.

DENSITY   the degree of opacity of a negative or a positive transparency.

DEPTH or IN-DEPTH REPORTING   the gathering and writing of background material for a news feature intended to round out information given in straight news reports.

DESCENDERS   1. the lines or loops of type that extend below the baseline of letters.   2. the letters themselves, as lower case g, j, p, etc.

DIAMOND★   A small size type, approximately 4½ point.

DIE CUT   paper that has been cut into a special shape or design with thin, shaped blades, or the cut-out hole that is left after such a piece has been removed.

DIE STAMPING   an intaglio method of printing on cards, letterheads, leather, etc. by means of a metal engraving.

DIGEST   a pocket-size magazine containing material, often condensed, reprinted from other sources.

DINGBAT   a decorative type element, as a bullet or star.

DIRECT MAIL   designating an advertising service that sends advertising or promotional literature directly to the prospective consumer by mail.

DIRTY   designating copy or proof that has had many changes, deletions, interlinear additions, etc., so that it is difficult to read; foul.

DISPLAY TYPE   large size type, often specially designed, and composed specifically to attract attention, as for advertising or headlines: oppdsed to *body type* (see BODY, sense 3).

DISTRIBUTE   to place type and other type elements back in cases after use.

DISTRICT MAN   a reporter who has a specific beat.

DOCTOR BLADE★   a metal device that wipes ink off the nonprinting surface of intaglio plates.

DODGE   in photography, to shade portions of a negative during printing, to prevent that part from becoming too dark: sometimes accomplished by rapid movements of a cardboard disk (*dodger*), or by chemical means: the process is called *dodging*. Opposed to BURN IN.

DOT   the individual printing element of a halftone plate.

DOT PATTERN (or FORMATION)   on a halftone negative or plate, the arrangement of different size dots formed by photographing through the screen: there are 22,500 dots to the square inch when a 150-line screen is used: see SCREEN.

DOUBLE DAGGER   a reference mark (‡); diesis.

*Dot pattern. Area enclosed by white lines in upper
picture has been enlarged to show halftone dot pattern.*

DOUBLE SPREAD   two facing pages made up as a single unit of editorial matter, often a pictorial layout with pictures extending across the gutters: sometimes shortened to *spread*. If in the center of a magazine, signature, etc., called *center spread*.

DOUBLET   1. type matter set by mistake a second time. 2. a newspaper item, paragraph, filler, etc. printed a second time in the same edition: also called *double* or *dupe*.

DOUBLE TRUCK   in advertising, two facing pages, usually in the center of a newspaper section or magazine signature, made up as a single unit and often containing pictorial matter that extends across the gutters.

DOWN STYLE   indicating printed matter that is styled with a minimum use of capital letters: see UP STYLE.

DRAGON'S BLOOD   a red resinous powder used in photoengraving as an acid resist on the sides of lines and dots to prevent undercutting, and on the relief printing surface to prevent further acid bite. See entry for RESIST.

DROP FOLIO   a FOLIO (sense 6) printed at the foot of a page.

DROPHEAD   the headline beneath a banner relating to the same story: also called *hanger, read out*. It is sometimes called a *dropline* or *deck head* when it is indented.

DROPOUT   a halftone plate on which the screen dots have been removed in the highlight portions; highlight halftone; facsimile.

DRUMBEATER   a press agent.

DRY OFFSET   a printing method in which a right-reading image from a cylinder plate prepared by relief printing (*patrix*) is offset to a rubber-covered blanket and
transferred from there to the paper. The relief plates are
usually prepared by photoengraving. Used for long-run
line or halftone printing, as revenue stamps. Eliminates
the need of water, as in conventional offset. Also called
high-etch, and in England, *dry relief offset.*

DRYPOINT   1. a method of engraving with a fine, hard
needle on a copper plate. A fine roughness called the *burr*
builds up along the edges of the incised lines. This holds
more ink than the clean lines of a line engraving or etching, and gives the print a characteristic soft line. Not
suitable for long runs, as the burr wears down. Can be
combined with *aquatint.*   2. the needle used for this.
3. the engraving produced, or a print taken from this.
Distinguished from LINE ENGRAVING, ETCHING.

DUMMY   1. a simulated magazine, booklet, book, etc.
with the correct number of (usually blank) pages, made
up into the size, format and general appearance desired
in the projected publication.   2. a similar set of pages,
but with the general layout of each page indicated; artwork is sketched or blueprints pasted in, proofs of type
are pasted into place, etc.

DUOTONE★   the printing of a halftone by the use of
plates in two colors, usually a color and black, which
blend to make a third color.[20]

DUPE 1. a duplicate or carbon copy. 2. copy that appears more than once in the same issue: also called *doublet*.

DUPLEX 1. a linecaster matrix with two forms of the same letter on it. 2. paper with a different color, texture, etc. on either side.

DWELL the brief moment in the process of letterpress printing when the paper comes into contact with the type.

EAR a small box in a upper corner of the front page: it may carry the weather report, the newspaper's slogan, etc.

EDITION 1. the copies of a book produced from one major setting of type, sometimes over a period of years; there may be *reprints* or subsequent *impressions* from the same type, or *revisions*, with changes within the existing pages, but the book remains the same *edition* until the type is completely reset. 2. a copy belonging to such a printing [first *edition*]. 3. same as ISSUE (for periodicals). 4. one of two or more issues of a newspaper or periodical coming out at a single publication time: different editions with some changes may be printed for appearance at succeeding times, or varied for different geographic areas.

EDITORIAL 1. designating all matter in a publication that is not advertising. 2. a column or page in which the editor expresses the policy of the paper or magazine as he comments on the news of the day or matters of current interest.[21] In former years, a newspaper policy reflected the opinions of the owner or publisher, and this is still true of small papers. But nowadays complete editorial freedom is often granted to editors of any of several papers of differing political or social views owned by the same publisher. *Editorializing* is the insertion of editors' or reporters' opinions in news stories or in articles that are conventionally supposed to be objective.

ELECTROTYPE a duplicate relief printing form, produced by electrolysis, as by depositing copper on a matrix of the original. The matrix may be wax, lead, or plastic, and the electrotype may be copper, nickel, or occasionally, steel: it is backed up with type metal when it is to be used. Electrotypes are durable, and used for long runs, as in book publishing.

ELITE a size of typewriter character that measures 12 characters to the inch: distinguished from PICA.

EM 1. the square dimension of a type body of any size: so called because the capital M nearly approximates this measure: used as a unit of measure. A 3-em space is a piece of spacing material that measures 3 to an em (i.e., each 3-em space measures $\frac{1}{3}$ of an em) ; a 5-em space measures 5 to an em, or $\frac{1}{5}$ of an em; etc. 2. loosely, a pica em (12 points) : used as a unit of width, but considered by many to be an inaccurate usage.

EMBOSS to raise paper in a relief pattern by the use of a die: if done without ink, called *blind embossing*.

EM DASH   a dash the length of an em in the point size being used: in copy or on proofs designated $\frac{1}{M}$.

EMERALD★   British name for a size of type, approximately 6½ point.

EM SPACE   a space the width of an em of the point size being used, accomplished by inserting an em quad (mutton quad). A 3-em space means ⅓ of an em, "4 to em" means ¼ of an em, etc., and is used to designate spacing material of these widths.

EN   one-half the width of the em of the same font.

EN DASH   a dash the length of an en in the point size being used: in copy or on proof designated $\frac{1}{N}$: used to separate figures, etc.

END MATTER   same as BACK MATTER.

END PAPER   a folded leaf, one half of which (*paste-down*) is pasted to the inside cover of a book; the other (*lining page*) forms the first (or last) page of the book: also called *end leaf*.[22]

ENGLISH★   1. a medium-large size type, approximately 14 point: see also COLUMBIAN.   2. a smooth, but not glossy, finish of book paper.

ENTROPY   in communications theory, a measure of efficiency in the communications of messages of a given system.

ERRATA   a printed list of printing errors, each referred to its page, inserted at the back of a book, or occasionally at the beginning: with its corrections, called *corrigenda*.

ETAOINSHRDLU   the line of type that results when a typesetter strikes each key in order going down the first and then the second row of keys vertically on a linecaster. Sometimes used to make a slug to set off material; it is not intended to appear in print.

EXCELSIOR★   the smallest size type, 3 point.[23]

EXPANDED   designating a typeface that is wider than the standard type of the same design [Century *Expanded*]: sometimes called *extended*. Opposed to CONDENSED.

FACE   1. the printing surface of a piece of type, halftone plate, or other printing element. See illustration for TYPE. 2. a typeface class or race (as roman, italic), family (as Caslon, Baskerville), or weight (often in combination, as *lightface, boldface*). 3. (a) the printed or inscribed side of a leaf, document, etc.   (b) the side of a printed sheet considered to be the main side.   4. the front of a book, dust jacket, etc.   5. the coated side of a film, or sensitized side of a photosensitized plate.   6. to place opposite a page: an illustration *faces* the opposite page.

FACER   a book page opposite the title page on which is a list of books by the same author or publisher: also called *book card*, (*ad* or *advertising*) *card page, card plate*, and *face-title*.

FACSIMILE★ 1. see HIGHLIGHT HALFTONE. 2. a process of transmitting and reproducing a newspaper, photographs, or other graphic material by radio. A scanner converts the matter into electrical impulses, which are reconverted and recorded by a stylus at the receiving point.

FAIR COMMENT as a defense of libel: the statement must concern a matter of public interest; it must be fair, and not malicious; and it must be comment and not an allegation of fact.[24]

FAMILY subdivision of a class of type, divided into SERIES. Type families are known by their trade names.[25]

FARM OUT to turn over a part of a publishing process, as linecasting, binding, etc. to another company.

FAT 1. same as EXPANDED (type). 2. that may be set quickly: said of copy, a page, etc. that is to be set with much leading, for which there is already some standing type, or that will have illustrations (*fat matter, a fat take, a fat page*): also spelled *phat*. 3. said of a line that cannot be set in the allotted space.

FEATURE an article or story, usually with human interest, often giving background information about news. It is usually intended to be of more lasting interest than an news item, and may or may not be written for publication on a specified date.

FEATURIZE to rewrite or enlarge a news story into a feature.

FEEDBACK 1. return of a small portion of the output of a computer, circuit, etc. to the input in order to correct, control, or sustain operation. 2. reader or audience response to a message.

FEET the bases on which a piece of type stands, divided by the GROOVE.[26] See illustration for TYPE.

FELT SIDE the side of paper next to the felt in manufacturing; the right side: opposite of WIRE SIDE.

FILE 1. to submit news copy to a newspaper, as by a reporter, especially a correspondent in another city or country. 2. to transmit copy by wire, telephone, cable, etc., as by a news service. 3. to keep back issues of a newspaper, or other material, for reference.

FILE 13, CIRCULAR FILE wastepaper basket.

FILLER 1. a secondary news item that may be placed anywhere on the page. 2. a short item, often timeless and from a stock kept on file, used to fill up a column.[27]

FIVE W'S AND THE H who, what, when, where, why, and how: the questions that should be answered in the conventional lead of a news story.

FIXING BATH the photographic bath that makes the picture permanent by toughening the gelatin film and rinsing away the remainder of the unaltered silver salts. HYPO is the most commonly used fixing agent (or, popularly, *fixer*).

FLACK★ 1. a press agent. 2. to serve as a press agent.

FLAG★   the nameplate of a newspaper on the front page; logo: distinguished from MASTHEAD.

FLAT   1. a number of negatives or positives assembled on a glass plate for platemaking.   2. a printing plate bearing a number of halftone or line images before they are sawed up into individual cuts.

FLATBED PRESS   any printing press in which the type forms lie flat.

FLEURON   a type ornament that is a stylized flower, usually cast in long rows to be used as borders: sometimes called *flower*.[28]

FLEXOGRAPHY   a high-speed rotary letterpress that uses flexible rubber plates: used for packaging and commercial products, ranging from hard-surfaced papers, plastics, foil, etc. to soft facial tissues.[29]

FLONG★   a sheet of papier-mâché used to make a stereotype matrix.

FLOWER   a type ornament: see FLEURON.

FLUBDUB   a decorative type element for ornamentation; dingbat.

FLUSH   set even with the margin, as *flush left, flush right*. Said of copy typed or set without paragraph indentions, or of subheads, or of copy in general.

FLYLEAF   a blank page at the front or back of a book.

F-NUMBER   the ratio of a camera lens aperture to focal distance: the smaller the number, the shorter exposure required.

FOG INDEX   a readability formula devised by Robert Gunning, 1959.

FOLDER   an advertising or promotional leaflet made from sturdy stock folded one or more times in any of a variety of patterns, but not stitched.[30]

FOLIO   1. a sheet of paper folded once.   2. a book, manuscript, etc. made up of these sheets.   3. the largest size of book commonly made, approximately 12″ x 19″.   4. a page in a book.   5. a size of paper, 17″ x 22″.   6. a page number, usually printed in the top margin: a number at the foot of the page is a *drop folio*.   7. a line or box, usually at the top of the page, containing a newspaper's name, date, page number, etc. Page one folio also contains volume number, year of publication, edition designation, and sometimes price, phone number, city, and state, but usually omits the name of the paper which is in the flag directly above.

FOLLOW   1. a later news story based on one previously published: also *follow-up* (*story*).   2. a sidebar.

FOLO   1. same as FOLLOW or FOLLOW-UP.   2. a clipping of a story from a previous issue, kept in a special file (or pile), that must be followed up in the current issue. 3. a tag at the end of a news story indicating that another installment in a series about the same subject will be printed in the following issue: opposite of PRECEDE (sense 2).

FONT★   type characters of one size of a given series along with spacing material of the same size. The number of characters in a font depends upon the face and its use.

FOREWORD   1. introductory material preceding a book, written by someone other than the author: distinguished from PREFACE.   2. loosely, a short preface.

FORM   type, and sometimes other printing elements, for a page or signature, locked up in a chase and ready for printing or for the preparation of duplicate printing plates.

FORMAT   the size, shape, and general physical characteristics of a publication.

FORWARDING   the steps in bookbinding following the sewing of the signatures together (or gluing, in perfect binding), but before casing-in.

FOTO   a photograph.

FOTOSETTER   a trademark for a machine that composes type photographically, but uses circulating matrices, as an Intertype.

FOUL   designating proof that has been marked for many changes so that it is difficult to read.

FOUNDRY TYPE   individual pieces of type for hand-setting: they are made of hard metal and intended for repeated use, rather than being remelted after use, as linecaster slugs or Monotype (*machine type*).

FOURDRINIER designating a paper-making machine that turns out paper in a continuous roll: developed in the early nineteenth century by, and named after, Sealy and Henry Fourdrinier.

FOURTH ESTATE★ the press; journalism or journalists.

FREE-LANCER★ a writer who has no long-term contracts or agreements with publications to buy his stories, articles, poetry, etc.: his mode of working is *free-lancing*.

FRISKET★ 1. originally, on a platen press, a thin frame between the tympan and form to hold a sheet in place. 2. protective paper stretched over a part of a form to prevent that section from printing. 3. a protective mask with cut-out areas through which the retouching of photographs or artwork with an airbrush is done, or through which parts of printing plate are worked upon.

FRONT MATTER material at the beginning of a book, before the main body: it may include title page, half title, frontispiece, table of contents, list of illustrations, preface, foreword, introduction, acknowledgments, etc.: also written *frontmatter,* and also called *preliminaries* or *fore matter*.

FUDGE★ a last-minute news item inserted in a newspaper: the hole left for its insertion is called a *fudge box* (or *column*). The *fudge box* is also the box attached to a linecaster in which fudge matter is put, then detached and sent to the pressroom for insertion in the plate: also called *jigger*.

FURNITURE   large spacing material: pieces of wood or metal, less than type-high and made in multiples of picas, for filling out spaces within a form.

FUTURE BOOK   an editor's calendar of upcoming events that will have to be covered on specific dates.

GAFFOON   a sound-effects man in radio or television.

GALLEY   1. a shallow, three-sided metal tray used to hold composed type.   2. the container into which linecaster slugs drop after casting.   3. short for GALLEY PROOF.

GALLEY PROOF   a proof taken from composed type in the galley, to allow for corrections before it is made up into pages.

GAMMA ALPHA CHI   advertising sorority, founded in 1920.

GANG   designating a negative or plate with several images that have been stripped together for printing at one time.

GARBLE   1. mixed-up, unintelligible copy transmitted and received on a teletype machine or cast on a linecaster, usually because of mechanical difficulties.   2. to make a message unintelligible.

GATEFOLD   a folded page or insert in a publication that is larger than the page and is unfolded to be read or seen.

GATEKEEPER   a person, agency, organization, etc., that has the power to let through or withold news, messages, information, etc.[31]

GATHERING   the collection, by machine or by hand, of the printed signatures or sheets of a book, booklet, etc. in the proper order: distinguished from COLLATING.

GAUGE PIN   a metal device used to hold sheets of paper in place on a platen press.

GAZETTE★   a newspaper: now used chiefly in newspaper names.

GEM★   a small size type, approximately 4 point.

GENERIC LEAD   same as BLIND LEAD.

GHOSTWRITER   a writer who composes work to be credited to someone else: his work is *ghostwriting*.

GILDING   the process of applying gold on book edges.

GLOSSY   1. a photographic print with glossy finish: opposed to MATTE.   2. a magazine printed on glossy-coated stock: see SLICK.

GOBO   1. a black screen used to shield a camera lens from bright light.   2. a screen used to shield a microphone from unwanted noise.

GOLDENROD (PAPER)   an opaque orange paper that is used as a backing for negatives on an offset flat.

GOTHIC   1. formerly, a kind of black letter type.   2. simple block lettering, usually sans serif, used in headings, advertising, and display, but seldom in body type.

GRAF   paragraph.

GRAIN   1. the direction in which paper fibers lie.[32] Direction of the grain can be determined by folding the paper: if it creases smoothly, it has been folded with the grain. 2. the degree of fineness of a photographic print, usually in proportion to how much it is enlarged. It is *grainy* if the image is broken up into fine segments. *Graininess* is sometimes deliberately developed for special effects.

GRAVER   a cutting or engraving tool, such as a burin.

GRAVURE   1. commercial intaglio printing, from plates prepared by a photomechanical process, using screened CARBON TISSUE; the ink is applied to minute wells or depressions of varying depths in the surface of the plate. 2. work done by this process.   3. short for PHOTOGRAVURE or ROTOGRAVURE.   4. loosely, any of several intaglio processes.[33]

GREAT PRIMER★   a large size type, 18 point.

GRIPPERS   metal fingers on a press cylinder that hold paper sheets while they are being printed: work done on sheet-fed presses must have an extra margin for the grippers.

GROOVE   the hollow depression on the base of a piece of type. The type stands on FEET, and the groove is the division between the feet. See illustration for TYPE.

GUILLEMETS   quotation marks (« ») used in French printing: called *duckfoot quotes* in England.

GUTTER   1. the white space of the inside margins of two facing pages, the area in which the publication is bound: also called *back margins*.   2. same as RIVER.

GUTTER POSITION   the position of an advertisement on the gutter column of a publication; considered to be a poor position.

GUTTER RECORDS   crime news.

HACK (WRITER)   a writer who is willing to take any assignment for any publication.

HAIRLINE   1. a fine-line stroke in artwork, or on a letter, as a thin stroke on a modern roman letter, connecting thicker strokes.   2. the thinnest rule in letterpress, used for borders, underscoring (*hairscoring*), etc.

HALF-DIAMOND   a style of indention in which each successive line is shortened equally at both ends: also called *inverted pyramid*.

HALF-ROUND   a stereotype plate curved to fit on the rotary press: also called *curved plate*.

HALF TITLE   1. the title of a book on a page alone, preceding the title page: also called *bastard title, fly title, mock title*.   2. the title of a book on a page alone, preceding the opening page of the first chapter.   3. the title of a book at the top of the first page of the first chapter.

HALFTONE   a printing plate, or the picture printed from it, made by exposing a continuous-tone negative through a screen, resulting in a plate with a large number of dots of varying sizes. The size screen, and thus the number of dots, is chosen largely by determining the kind of paper on which the picture will be reproduced: see also SCREEN.

HANDOUT   a release given out by a press agent, government agency, public relations or advertising personnel, etc.

HANDSET   said of type that is composed from individual types, rather than being *machine-set,* as by a linecaster.

HANGER   same as DROPHEAD.

HANGING INDENTION   a style of indention in which the first line is set full width, with the successive lines equally indented. This copy is set in the hanging indention style. It may also be called *reverse indention,* as it is the opposite of the conventional indention for a paragraph.[34]

HARLEQUINS   decorative type elements that are somewhat black and heavy, shaped like diamonds, half-circles, etc.

HEADBAND   1. a narrow strip of cotton cloth pasted at top and bottom of the back of a book for reinforcement before it is cased in.   2. an ornamental border at the beginning of a chapter or top of a page.

HEADING   any material set at the beginning of copy to identify it, as a headline, subhead, chapter head, title of a table, etc.

HEADNOTE   a short note, often set in italics, accompanying the heading, and giving information about the author or the story.

HEIGHT-TO-PAPER   the standard height of type from feet to face, .9186 in.

HELLBOX   a container in the composing room or printshop where used type, to be remelted, is thrown.

HIGH-ETCH   see DRY OFFSET.

HIGHLIGHT   the bright, or most nearly white, portions of a halftone or photograph.

HIGHLIGHT HALFTONE   a halftone in which the screen dots are removed photographically or by burnishing, so that the highlight portions are completely white; dropout; facsimile.

HOLD or HOLD FOR RELEASE   a direction to indicate copy is not to be printed until a specified time (*release time*) or under specified conditions. Abbreviated HFR.

HOLE   a blank space in a form or on a page, sometimes left for copy not yet available, sometimes deliberately reserved for last-minute news. See also NEWS HOLE.

HORSE   to read proof alone, comparing it directly with copy, and without the aid of a copyholder.

HOT TYPE (or METAL)   type or linecaster slugs cast from molten metal: see also COLD TYPE.

HOUSE AD in a magazine, an advertisement within the magazine for itself or another magazine by the same publisher.

HOUSE ORGAN a company newspaper, magazine, or sometimes, newsletter.

HOUSE STYLE the style used in a given publishing house for all of its publications. Particulars are usually specified in a stylebook.

HYPO sodium thiosulfate, a commonly used fixing agent in photography.

IMPOSING STONE the flat metal-topped, stone, or marble table on which the printer (*stoneman*) makes up the page form and locks it into the chase. When type is *on the stone* it is set and ready for use.

IMPOSITION the proper placement of forms for several pages to be printed on one sheet so that, when folded into a signature, they will follow in the right order.

IMPRESSION 1. the act, moment, or degree of the pressure or touching of printing elements against the paper. 2. the piece of printing resulting from this. 3. the copies of a book printed without alteration of pages but at a different time, as a second or third impression of an EDITION.

IMPRINT the name and city of the publisher printed at the bottom of the title page of a book.

INCUNABULA   early printing, produced in the fifteenth century.

INDIA PAPER   a thin, strong, opaque paper used for Bibles, dictionaries, etc.

INDICIA   1. a postal marking with information indicating that postage has been paid, as by a postal permit, printed on a publication, advertising folder, label, wrapper, etc.   2. (a) a block of type, usually smaller than body type, printed as a heading for a review of a book, containing title, name of author, publication data, etc. (b) a block like this as a heading for a review of a motion picture, or any like material.   3. publication data given in a bibliography, footnote, etc.

INFERIOR   designating letters or figures smaller than the type used, that appear below the line of type$_{156}$: also called *subscripts*.

INITIAL LETTER   the large first letter used at the beginning of a body of set type for emphasis or decoration. *Up, rising,* or *stickup* means that the letter aligns with the body type on its baseline; *down, inset, dropped,* or *sunken* means that the top of the letter aligns with the top of the first line. A two-line initial occupies the space of two lines of body type.

INK FOUNTAIN   a reservoir for ink on a printing press, with a device to regulate the flow of ink onto the printing rollers.

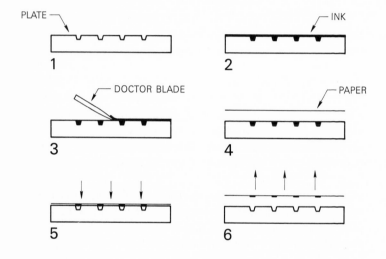

Intaglio printing

INTAGLIO★ 1. a printing method in which the image is carried in incised lines, as by engraving or etching: distinguished from RELIEF, LITHOGRAPHY. 2. a plate produced by this method, or a print from this.

INTERNATIONAL NEWS SERVICE a news service founded in 1906 by William Randolph Hearst, and merged with United Press in 1958 to form United Press International. Wire service commenced in 1915.

INTERTYPE a trademark for a linecasting machine.

INTRODUCTION   1. introductory material leading into the subject, written by an author to precede the main text of his book; it may be part of the front matter, or presented as the first part of the text.   2. a foreword written by someone other than the author to introduce the author and his work to the reader.   3. a book intended to present the basic aspects of a subject or course of study.

INVERTED PYRAMID   1. form of journalistic writing in which the major points of the story are told in the first sentence or paragraph, with details expounded in descending order of importance:[35] developed on the theory that many newspaper readers do not read beyond the first one or two paragraphs.   2. a bank of newspaper headlines in which the top head is set in large type, and each line below in successively smaller type.   3. same as HALF-DIAMOND (indention).

ISLAND POSITION   the location of an advertisement completely surrounded by editorial matter: an advantageous position because the ad is not in competition with nearby ads.

ISSUE   all of the copies and editions of a publication produced from essentially one setting of type, and available at the same date: see also EDITION.

ITALIC   a delicate, slanted form of type used to indicate that a word or phrase is foreign, or for emphasis: most roman types have a companion italic.

JEFF★ a game played by throwing em quads like dice: the player who throws the greatest number of em quads with nick side up wins.

JIM DASH a hairline centered between the decks of a headline, or between a headline and story, or between short items in the same column.

JOB CASE a shallow tray for type, usually holding both upper and lower case characters: see CALIFORNIA JOB CASE.

JOB WORK or **JOBBING** miscellaneous commercial printing. A printshop that does this kind of work exclusively is called a *job shop*.

JOG to straighten or align the edges of piled sheets of paper, usually by fanning out so air can get between the sheets, then shaking down on a flat surface: often done by a machine (*jogger*).

J-SCHOOL journalism school.

JUGGLED SLUGS lines that have been reinserted in the wrong position after being corrected and recast on a linecaster.

JUMP 1. to continue a story or article on another page or in another column. 2. the continued portion of the story: sometimes called BREAK.

JUMP HEAD a headline for the portion of a story or article that is continued on another page.

JUMPLINE the continuation line at the bottom of a column or page of the first portion of a jump story (continued on page 34), or at the top of a jump (continued from page 1).

JUSTIFY to add spacing to lines of type so that all lines are of equal length. Done automatically by linecasters, Monotype casters, and justifying typewriters.

JUSTOWRITER a trademark for a set of typewriters that turns out justified copy: when material is typed onto the keyboard of the first, it turns out punched tape, which activates the second.

KAPPA TAU ALPHA journalism fraternity, founded in 1910.

KEEP STANDING a direction to the printer to hold type after a printing job has been completed. Opposite of KILL.

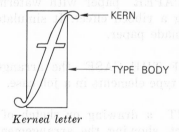

Kerned letter

KERN the part of the face of a piece of type that extends beyond the body.

KEYLINE a line at the bottom of a book page explaining symbols used.

KICKER a short line set in smaller type over a headline, containing a few words to identify the subject (or writer, if it is a column), or entice the reader; overline; also called *teaser, eyebrow, highline,* etc. A *reverse kicker* or *barker* is one in which one word or a short phrase is set in large type over a regular headline in smaller type.

KILL 1. a direction not to use copy. 2. a direction to distribute the type and discard the cuts, etc. from a form. Opposite of KEEP STANDING.

KING FEATURES SYNDICATE the largest of the features syndicates, serving nearly 1,800 newspapers. It carries a great number of features, as columns, cartoons, comic strips, fiction, games, patterns, etc.

KISS IMPRESSION the ideal impression of printing element and paper, neither too light nor too heavy.

LAID PAPER paper with watermarked parallel lines, giving a ribbed effect. It simulates the texture of old handmade paper.

LAY OF THE CASE the arrangement of letters and other type elements in a job case.

LAYOUT a drawing or sketch of a proposed printing project, showing the arrangement of individual units and giving specifications; working diagram of a job: see also ROUGH, COMPREHENSIVE.

LEAD (ledd) 1. (a) a strip of type metal, about shoulder-height of type, used for interlinear spacing. (b) metal the size of a lead that is cast as part of a type. The thickness of leads is measured in points, with 2-point the most commonly used. Leaded matter is considered to be leaded 2 points unless otherwise specified. 2. to put leads between lines of type.

LEAD (lēd) 1. the first sentence or paragraph of a news story, traditionally containing the five W's and H: see also BLIND LEAD. 2. the most important news story of the day. 3. in wire news service, (a) an entire news story [a new *lead* will move shortly]. (b) a part of a story: there may be an original lead, a first lead, second lead (of the same story). As the new leads move, each one incorporates new information and further detail. 4. to feature a particular item or article in a news story [to *lead* a shooting in the story of a riot].

LEADER 1. the leading news article in a newspaper. 2. in England, an editorial. 3. one of a series of dots or hyphens extending across a page to lead the eye to corresponding matter, as in an index or tabular matter.

LEAD-IN 1. a few words at the beginning of a paragraph, set in a different kind of type from the body of the text, as small capitals or boldface. 2. a provocative beginning of a piece of writing.

LEADING (ledding) spacing between lines of type matter, accomplished by inserting leads, or by using type that is already leaded.

LEAN   1. same as CONDENSED (type).   2. said of copy that is fairly difficult to set, and may be unprofitable as job work: opposed to FAT, PHAT.

LEGEND   1. a title, short description, or identification of subjects under an illustration; cutline.   2. a key to a map, usually inset.

LEGIBILITY   the relative ease or difficulty of reading any given material, considered from its physical aspects. Factors may include choice of typeface, amount of white space, blackness of ink and whiteness of paper—page design in general: distinguished from READABILITY.

LEGMAN   a newspaper reporter who goes out to cover stories on the scene, phoning periodically with news to be handled in the office by the REWRITE MAN. Also called *legger* (rare).

LENS-LOUSE   a person who is greedy for publicity, and edges his way into news photographs, or in front of a television camera.[36]

LETTERPRESS   1. a printing method in which the image is carried on raised surfaces, as set type, halftone plates, etc.; relief printing.   2. printed matter produced by this method.   3. in England, text, as distinguished from illustrations.

LETTERSPACING   the addition of extra spacing between letters, either for a better appearance, or to fill out a line. Occasionally called *interspacing*.

LIBEL   a false accusation of (1) insanity, or contagious or loathsome disease, (2) crime, (3) inability to conduct one's business or profession, or (4) anything that would bring public hatred, ridicule, or contempt.

LIBEL, DEFENSE OF   (1) truth, (2) fair comment, (3) privileged communication. See entries for FAIR COMMENT and PRIVILEGED COMMUNICATION.

LIFT   the number of sheets that may be conveniently lifted from a press at one time.

LIGATURE   two or more letters designed to fit closely together, and cast on a single type body. The most commonly used are fi, fl, ff, ffi, ffl. These ligatures are designed to prevent breaking of kerns. Others, as œ and æ, are done to accommodate these conventional forms. Also designed as symbols for advertising, or to identify a wire service, etc.

LINECASTER or LINECASTING MACHINE   a typesetting machine that casts a complete, justified line of type on one slug: it is activated by a keyboard or by perforated tape previously punched out by keyboard operation.

LINE CUT   a photoengraving of a line drawing, with only solid lines and no intermediate tones: also called *line engraving:* distinguished from HALFTONE. A zinc etching is a line cut made on a zinc plate.

LINE GAUGE   a printer's ruler, marked in pica increments; pica rule.

LINING   the alignment of letters of different sizes or of different typefaces, on the *standard line:* types are cast commonly now with the standard line, so that different sizes of the same type design, or different designs of the same or different sizes, can be combined with a certainty that they will align on the baseline. Display type (in a *lining series*) ordinarily has a lower baseline than body type.

LINOTYPE★   a trademark for a linecasting machine, invented by Ottmar Mergenthaler in 1886.

LITERALS   type characters: to read proof for literals is to read letter for letter, watching for proper spelling, punctuation, etc., as well as for typos: formerly spelled *letterals.*

LITHOGRAPHY   a printing method in which the image is carried on a plane surface. The image is applied to a stone or metal plate with a greasy material; first water or an acid solution is applied, then ink; the ink adheres only to the greased surface. It was invented in 1799 by Alois Senefelder. See also OFFSET LITHOGRAPHY, PHOTO-LITHOGRAPHY.

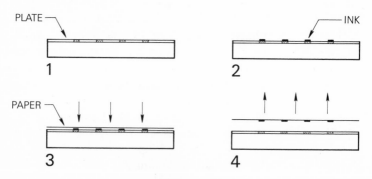

Lithography

LITTLE MAGAZINE a noncommercial magazine of limited circulation (5,000 or under), usually literary or political, and often unorthodox, sophisticated, and experimental.

LIVE 1. designating type that is still in use, or being held for future use; alive. 2. designating a sound system or microphone that is turned on; alive. 3. designating a broadcast of events as they occur, rather than recorded or taped at an earlier time.

LOBSTER TRICK★ 1. the shift in a newspaper or wire service office that takes in late night and early morning hours; graveyard shift; dog-watch; night side. 2. the skeleton staff in a newspaper office from the time the paper has been put to bed until work on the next issue begins. Also *lobster-shift.*

LOCKUP the process of locking (with a *quoin*) type elements into a chase to hold them securely for printing or preparation of duplicate printing plates.

LOGOTYPE (more commonly LOGO) 1. a type containing a syllable, word, or words (as *ble, the*) : distinguished from LIGATURE, which has its letters tied together. 2. a printing plate that contains (a) a company's name or trademark, used in advertising; (b) a newspaper's nameplate (FLAG), sometimes in miniature to be used in the MASTHEAD; (c) a signature, etc.

LONG PRIMER★ a medium-large size type, 10 point.

LOWER CASE the small letters in a font, formerly kept in the lower of two type cases facing the compositor: distinguished from UPPER CASE, the capital letters.

LOWER CASE ALPHABET (LENGTH)   the amount of linear space in points occupied by the lower case alphabet, used as a unit of measurement in copyfitting: each size of type has its own *lca.*

LOW TO PAPER   designating type or other printing elements that have become worn down so they are no longer type-high.

LUDLOW   a trademark for a machine that casts slugs from handset matrices assembled in a special composing stick. It casts display type, usually 18-point or over, for headings, advertisements, etc.

MACHINE-SET   said of type that is set by a typesetting machine, as opposed to HANDSET.

MACKLE★   a double or blurred impression in printing.

MAGAZINE★   1. a periodical, usually paper-covered, containing articles, stories, poems, etc., by different authors, often illustrated, and also often containing advertisements. It may be directed at the general public, or at a special-interest group or particular age group.   2. the receptacle in a typesetting machine that holds the circulating matrices.   3. the film container in a camera.

MAILER   1. a news story or feature sent out by a news agency or wire news service by mail rather than by wire. Many small agencies use mailers exclusively.   2. an advertising leaflet to be sent out by direct mail. If it is intended to be included with regular mail, also called *envelope stuffer.*

MAJUSCULE★   a capital letter.

MAKEREADY   the process of making a final adjustment of the printing and impression surfaces of a press so that a uniform impression will result: accomplished by the use of various leveling devices, application of overlays, underlays, etc.

MAKE THE EAGLE SCREAM   to print in large, bold headlines.

MAKEUP   the assembling of set type, plates, and other printing elements into page form.

MAKEUP RULE   a small steel rule with a projection at the end, used to separate lines of type.

MASS COMMUNICATIONS   messages, or the science or techniques of communicating messages, to the general public, by means of the mass media.[37]

MASS MEDIA   all methods of communication designed to reach the general public: newspapers, periodicals, radio, television, films, books, etc.[38]

MASTHEAD★   1. the identification matter printed in each issue of a newspaper or periodical, usually on the editorial page, stating the title, publisher, management, place of publication, rates, and often circulation figures: distinguished from NAMEPLATE. 2. loosely, same as NAMEPLATE: considered by some to be an inaccurate usage.

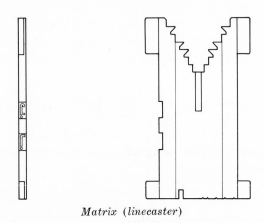

Matrix (linecaster)

MATRIX (plural *matrices*)   1. the mold from which type characters are cast in foundry type, Monotype, or line-casting machines.   2. the mold, of papier-mâché, wax, plastic, plaster, etc. taken from a type or plate form, and from which a stereotype or electrotype plate may be cast. Often shortened to *mat*.

MATTE   a photographic print with a dull finish.

MCKITTRICK'S DIRECTORY   a directory listing advertising agencies in the United States, Canada, and some overseas countries.

MEAN LINE   the line that would appear to run along the top of the primary lower case letters (those without ascenders, as *aeiou*) : the upper limit of the X-HEIGHT of letters: opposed to BASELINE.

MEASURE   the width of a column or page, usually expressed in picas.

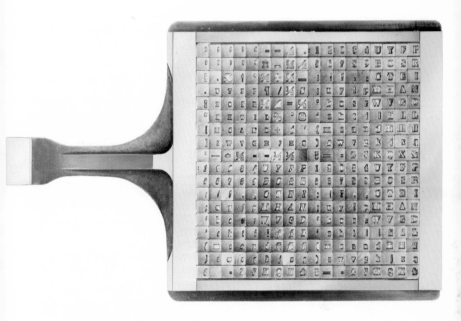

Monotype matrix case
(Courtesy American Typefounders Co., Inc.)

MECHANICAL   a finished piece of copy ready for photo-mechanical reproduction, with pictures, hand-lettering, typed copy or proofs of set type, etc. positioned correctly: if the elements are pasted into place, it may also be called a PASTE-UP.

MEDIUM (plural *media*)   1. a means of conveying an advertising message, as newspaper, magazine, radio, television, direct mail, etc.   2. any method of communication, as used for entertainment, conveying information, etc.   3. a size of paper, 19″ x 24″ for writing, 18″ x 23″ for printing.

MERIDIAN★   a very large size type, approximately 44 point.

METAL   1. type that has been set; composed type.   2. type metal.

MEZZOTINT   1. a very old fine-art etching process, invented by Ludwig von Siegen in 1643, in which the surface, of copper or steel, is burred (or *rocked*), then burnished slightly in some areas.   2. an etching produced by this process.

MILL   a typewriter (used especially in newspaper or wire service offices).

MILLINE   an agate line of space in one million copies of a publication: used to determine the *milline rate,* the cost of such a line. The *maximil* rate (short for *maximum milline rate*) is the highest rate charged for this space.

MINIKIN★   British name for the smallest size type, 3 point.

MINION★   a popular size of type, approximately 7 point.

MINIONETTE★   a size of type, approximately 6½ point.

MINUSCULE★   a lower-case letter.

MODERN   1. designating a roman type having straight serifs and marked variation in the strokes (hairlines, and thick stems), designed by Bodoni in 1783: see also OLD STYLE, TRANSITIONAL.   2. designating numerals that do not extend below the baseline.

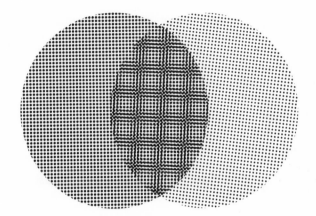

Moiré

MOIRÉ   a visual effect much like a moiré pattern (wavy lines), or sometimes alternate light and dark diamond-shaped areas, that often occurs if a halftone engraving is made of a halftone reproduction and the dot patterns coincide. It is undesirable in news photos, but its unusual appearance is used effectively in some photographic prints for art, advertising, etc.

MONK   an old term for a very black smudge or blotch of ink: a *friar* was a lighter ink blot.

MONOTYPE★ a trademark for a machine that casts individual type characters and assembles them into justified lines of a specified length: it is activated by perforated tape (RIBBON) produced on a companion keyboard machine. Invented by Tolbert Lanston, 1887.

MONTAGE a composite of many pictures, or parts of them, pasted up together and photographed: if photos are used, it is a *photomontage.*

MORDANT in etching, the acid or other corrosive used to "bite" the metal plate.

MORGUE the reference files or shelves of a newspaper, magazine, or other publication, where its collection of photographs, clippings, back numbers, and other reference materials are kept.

MOTIVATIONAL RESEARCH marketing and advertising research intended to determine consumers' motives for buying.

MOVABLE TYPE individual types, with each letter alone on its own body, that can be assembled, then reassembled into different words: invented by Johann Gutenberg about 1450.[39]

MOVE in wire news service, to transmit copy by wire.

MUCKRAKERS★ a group of crusading magazine journalists of the early 1900's. They included Ida Tarbell, Ray Stannard Baker, Upton Sinclair, Thomas Lawson, Burton J. Hendrick, Charles E. Russell, Lincoln Steffens, David Graham Phillips, and Samuel Hopkins Adams. Crusading magazines included *McClure's, Everybody's,* and *Collier's.*[40]

MULTILITH   a trademark for an offset printing machine for which the copy is prepared by typing or drawing, etc., directly onto thin metal lithographic plates.

MUST   1. copy that must be included in a certain edition of a publication: sometimes *musty:* see also BOM in list of abbreviations.   2. an instruction that copy may not be changed in any way.

MUTTON QUAD   an em quadrat.

NAMEPLATE   1. the name of a newspaper across the top of the front page; flag.   2. the plate from which this is printed.

NECK   the upright side of the projecting character on a piece of type between the counter (shoulder) and face: if the neck is beveled, it is called a BEVEL or BEARD, though the latter term often includes both the bevel and the shoulder adjacent to it.

NEMO★   a television or radio broadcast that originates outside of the station's studios.

NEWS AGENCY   an organization for gathering and distributing news, features, photographs, etc. to its subscribers.

NEWS AGENT   British term for NEWSDEALER (sense 1).

NEWSCAST   a radio or television broadcast of news.

NEWSDEALER 1. the owner or operator of a stand or store for the retail sale of newspapers, magazines, etc. 2. a distributor of periodicals.

NEWS FLASH 1. a news item sent by radio or telegraph. 2. a late news item, usually condensed, broadcast on radio or television.

NEWS HOLE space left for editorial matter after advertisements and standing matter have been allowed for.

NEWSHOUND a journalist; reporter or news photographer: sometimes *newshawk,* and feminine, *newshen.*

NEWSPAPER ENTERPRISE ASSOCIATION a combination news service and features syndicate, founded in 1902.

NEWSPRINT a rough, cheap paper, usually made from wood pulp, used for newspapers.

NEWSROOM 1. a room in a newspaper office where news is gathered in from outside sources and written or rewritten for the paper. 2. a room where news is written, edited, broadcast, etc. in a television or radio studio, or from which news is disseminated in an organizational or government building.

NEWSWORTHY timely and of sufficient interest to warrant space in a newspaper, mention on a newscast, etc.: often used to designate an item of special interest.

NICK the groove in one side of a piece of type by which it is identified according to font. See illustration for TYPE. When the type is set by hand, the nicks of the row are toward the compositor, and align as it lies in the composing stick. A piece of type from the wrong font shows up.

NIELSEN RADIO AND TELEVISION INDEX a rating of the popularity of shows, as determined by the A. C. Nielsen Company.

NIGHT SIDE 1. designating the staff of a newspaper or wire news service that works during the night. 2. the shift worked. See LOBSTER TRICK.

NIXIE a piece of direct mail that failed to reach the potential consumer because of an incorrect address.

NONPAREIL★ 1. a size of type, 6 point. 2. a 6-point slug, as used between newspaper columns. 3. a lineal unit of measurement, 6 points.

NUT QUAD an en quadrat.

OBIT an obituary; a notice or account of a person's death, often with a biography and list of survivors.

OCTAVO a book made up of leaves cut eight from a sheet; 16 pages measuring approximately 6″ x 9″; 8vo; 8°: see note at QUARTO.

ODDMENTS parts of a book that are not part of the text, as the title page, index, etc.

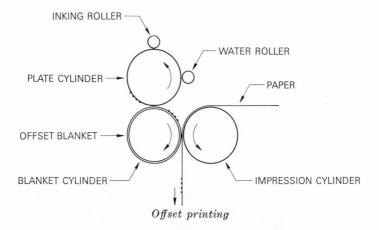

Offset printing

OFFSET   1. a printing method in which a right-reading image from a dampened planographic cylinder is transferred to a rubber blanket, and is from there offset onto the paper: in full, *offset lithography*. See also DRY OFFSET. 2. a smudge of ink transferred from a freshly printed sheet to the one next to it: prevented by a SLIPSHEET.

OLD ENGLISH   a style of black letter type; text.

OLD MAN, THE   the managing editor.

OLD STYLE   1. designating a roman type having bracketed serifs, and little variation in the strokes, as distinguished from MODERN. Among the Old Style typefaces are Caslon, Elzevir, Garamond, and Granjon.   2. designating numerals that have part of the 3, 4, 5, 7, and 9 extending below the baseline.

OPACITY   the property of a paper that determines whether or not print will show through from the other side or the next sheet.

OPAQUE   1. in photography (a) an opaque paint or other preparation used to *block out* parts of a negative or print. (b) to apply opaque.   2. not allowing print to show through: said of some paper.

OPEN   1. designating a newspaper that has little advertising, and thus as much or more room than is needed for news: sometimes *wide open:* opposite of TIGHT.   2. designating a magazine that has more than enough room for the material at hand.   3. designating a style of composition in which there is a relatively large amount of white space on the page.   4. set with leads between lines of type; not solid.   5. designating a style of punctuation in which as few punctuation marks as possible are used.

OPTICAL CENTER   the center of a page or sheet as it appears to the eye: it is approximately ⅛ above the geometric center.

OVERDEVELOP   to develop a photographic film or plate in too strong a developer, or to leave it in the developer too long.

OVERHEAD   see BACKBONE (sense 2).

OVERLAY   1. a patch or sheet of paper, usually tissue, affixed to the impression surface during letterpress makeready, to help obtain a uniform impression by making the printing element, or a portion of it, of the same height as the rest of the form.   2. a transparent flap over artwork, maps, offset lithography copy, etc. showing areas of color, details, additional or temporary lines, etc., and sometimes carrying instructions.

OVERLINE   1. a banner head set above the flag on a newspaper front page.   2. a one-line caption set above an illustration.   3. a kicker.

OVERPRINT   1. to print over or on top of a surface that has been previously printed.   2. the material or design so printed, or the item on which it is printed, as a postage stamp. Also called *surprint*.

OVERRUN   1. to shift words or letters from one line to another in making corrections or adding or deleting matter set in type.   2. copies of printed matter in excess of what was ordered: buyers are sometimes expected to accept up to 10% more copies than ordered if spoilage is not as great as anticipated: often used in plural, *overruns*.   3. paper cut and delivered in excess of the amount ordered.

OVERSET   matter set in type and not used: sometimes called *overs, overmatter*.

OVER-THE-TRANSOM   designating unsolicited material submitted to a publishing house, magazine, etc. by freelancers.

OVERWRITE   to write too much, or especially, to write in too much detail, or in language or style that is too ornate or literary for the subject matter or to suit publication policy.

OZALID   a trademark for a process of duplicating graphic material, or a semipermanent image produced by this process: often used for architectural renderings.

PAD   to make a story longer by adding extraneous details, adjectives, etc.

PAGE   1. one side of a leaf of a book, magazine, newspaper, etc.   2. loosely, the entire leaf, as in "turn the page."   3. the printing or writing on a page.   4. the type or other printing elements set and ready for the printing of a page.

PAGE PROOF   a proof pulled after printed matter has been made up into pages: distinguished from GALLEY PROOF.

PAGINATION   1. the system of numbering the pages of a book, magazine, etc.   2. the act of numbering such pages, or the numbers, symbols, letters, etc. used.   3. the number and arrangement of pages.

PALLET   a tool for printing letters on a book cover: also called a *typeholder*.[41]

PAMPHLET   a small, thin, unbound booklet, often with a self-cover, and with its leaves stitched or stapled together. Writers of political arguments who publish their treatises in this format are called *pamphleteers*.

PAN   to move a television or motion picture camera in a sweeping fashion, in order to follow a moving object or obtain a panoramic effect.

PANCHROMATIC   designating photographic film, plate, or emulsion that is sensitive to the light from all colors.

PAPER SIZES   Paper comes in standard size sheets, with the size determined by the intended use and thus the number of smaller sheets that it will be cut into. For example, the standard size sheet of bond paper that will be cut into 8½″ x 11″ sheets is usually 23″ x 35″, which will be cut into 8 sheets.[42] It is the largest standard size sheet referred to in figuring the BASIS WEIGHT, which see.

PARAGON★   a large size type, approximately 20 point. *Two-line paragon* is approximately 40 point.

PARALLAX   in photography, the difference between what is seen in the viewfinder and the scene taken in by the picture-taking lens, for which allowance must be made.

PARENS   parentheses.

PASTE-UP (or PASTEUP)   1. an arrangement of repro proofs, artwork, etc. on a page ready for photomechanical reproduction; mechanical.   2. a dummy with its elements pasted into place.   3. copy that has been pasted on a larger sheet so that it may be worked upon.   4. a book or other literary work made up by pasting together material previously published or used elsewhere.

PATENT INSIDES (or OUTSIDES)   features or other syndicated material that come to a newspaper already printed on inside (or first and last) pages; readyprint pages.

PEARL★   a small size type, approximately 5 point.

PEBBLING   a process of graining paper so that it has tiny irregularities or dimples.

PECULIARS   1. characters in a font of type that are seldom used: also *side sorts*.   2. type characters that bear
accents, as for setting phonetics or some languages, as
Hebrew, Scandinavian, Slavic, etc.

PEG   the essential feature in a news story, or at least the
leading human interest aspect on which a journalist may
pivot his story.

PERFECT BINDING   a process of gluing single sheets
of a book together and encasing it in a cover, without
stitching or sewing.

PERFECTING   the printing of the second side of a sheet:
also called *backing-up*.

PERFECTING PRESS   a rotary press that prints both
sides of a sheet in one pass through the press.

PERIODICAL   a publication that is produced at regular
intervals of more than one day, but less than a year: the
term is not used of newspapers, regardless of interval
between issues.

PHAT★   1. same as FAT.   2. to keep type standing in case
another printing is called for: type that is kept standing
is called *phatted type*.

PHOTOENGRAVING 1. a photomechanical process of producing relief printing plates. A negative of the original is made by a copying camera. If the image is a line drawing with no intermediate tones, the negative is made the same as any other photograph. A continuous-tone image is screened to produce a dot pattern: see HALF-TONE. The negative is placed on sensitized zinc or copper plates, and exposed to light; then the soluble portions of the sensitizing material not hardened on the plate by light are washed away. A chemical then etches away the nonprinting portions of the plate, leaving a raised surface to be inked and printed. 2. a printing plate produced by this method, or a print from this.

PHOTOGELATIN see COLLOTYPE.

PHOTOGRAVURE 1. fine arts intaglio printing from plates prepared by a photomechanical method. A film positive is exposed on CARBON TISSUE (unscreened), which is applied to a plate coated with minute granules of resin. A chemical etches away the metal of the areas to be printed, to varying depths.[43] 2. the intaglio plate made by this process. 3. the continuous-tone print produced from such a plate, with a typical satiny finish. Distinguished from GRAVURE and ROTOGRAVURE, which use a screen, and are used for high-speed printing methods.

PHOTOJOURNALISM 1. the art or profession of telling news by pictures, with or without accompanying text. The objective is the achievement of maximum narrative effect from photographs. 2. journalism in which pictures occupy more space than does the text, as in some magazines such as *Life* or *Look*.

PHOTOLITHOGRAPHY   1. a photomechanical process of producing lithographic printing plates. The negative is prepared in the same way as for photoengraving, placed on a sensitized zinc or aluminum plate, and exposed to light. The plate is then coated with a greasy ink. The soluble portions of the sensitizing material not hardened on the plate by the action of light are washed away, leaving the ink-covered image. The plate is printed by a lithographic or offset lithographic method, producing a *photolithograph*.

PHOTOMECHANICAL   designating any process by which material is prepared for printing by a photographic process. Copy may be prepared for any of the three types of printing: for relief—photoengraving; for lithography—photolithography, collotype; for intaglio—gravure, photogravure, rotogravure.

PHOTOSTAT   a trademark for a photographic copying machine, or a copy of material made by this machine: the latter is sometimes shortened to *stat*.

PI   jumbled and mixed-up type, as when a form is dropped and the type broken up.

PIC   picture(s).

PICA   1. a medium-large size type, 12 point.   2. a unit of lineal and type-page measurement (derived from the x-height of this size of type) of 12 points, or about ⅙ inch: distinguished from *em*.   3. a size of typewriter character that measures 10 characters to the inch: distinguished from ELITE.

PICA RULE   a printer's ruler, marked in pica increments; line gauge: also called *pica pole*.

PICKUP   1. type matter already set that is to be incorporated with fresh material.   2. in wire news service, an
earlier lead on a story, to be incorporated with a new
lead, or the particular point on the original copy where
the new material is to be inserted. To *pick up* is to start
at the point where copy was previously stopped.   3. the
place from which a remote broadcast originates.

PI DELTA EPSILON   journalism fraternity, founded in
1909.

PIECE FRACTIONS   figures (each on its own body) half
the depth of the size of type with which they are to be
printed, with a horizontal or slant line over the denomi-
nator so they may be made up into fractions: also called
split fractions.

PIGEONHOLE   too wide a space between printed words:
several of them falling nearly under each other in successive lines may cause a RIVER, which see.

PIG IRON   newspaper copy that is dull or serious.

PIN MARK   the round mark on the side of a piece of type,
made by the pin that ejects it from the mold when it is
cast. See illustration for TYPE.

PIPELINE   a person who is a direct source of information, but does not want his identity revealed.

PIX[44]   pictures.

PLAGIARISM   the copying of material written by another without permission or acknowledgment, with the
intention of claiming it as one's own.

PLANER   a flat block of wood used with a mallet to press type flat on its feet in the form during makeready.

PLANOGRAPHY or PLANOGRAPHIC PRINTING   1. any printing process from a plane surface, as distinguished from intaglio or relief. It includes lithography, offset lithography, collotype, etc.   2. work done by this process.   3. in common use, the simpler and less expensive form of photolithography.[45]

PLATEN PRESS   a relief printing press on which the type form is locked in a flat vertical position, and the paper carried on another flat surface, which is brought against the form with an action much like that of a clamshell.

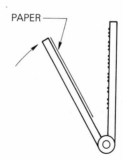

Platen press

PLAY   1. to determine which angle of a news story or feature should be the lead [how shall we *play* this story?].   2. to feature a particular item or angle in a news story.   3. to give more or less emphasis to a feature, news story, etc. by the manner in which it is displayed [to *play up* an item with big headlines, a prominent place on the page, illustrations, sidebars, etc.; to *play down* an item by giving it little space, perhaps on an inside page].

PLUG 1. (a) a book sold at a reduced price by a publisher after sales have fallen off: in plural, also *remainders*. (b) a defective book. 2. copy intended to be used for fillers. 3. a recommendation for a commercial product, performer, etc., given free in a radio or television show, newspaper column, etc.

POINT 1. a unit of type measurement, $\frac{1}{12}$ of a pica (about $\frac{1}{72}$ in.) : .01384 in foundry type, .014 on linecasting machines. 2. a period, or, sometimes, any punctuation mark.

POINT SYSTEM the system by which type and spacing material is made to exact measurement, and is designated by the number of points it measures: adopted in 1878 to make it possible to estimate accurately the space a given amount of type would occupy, or to interchange types from different foundries. Prior to this time, the different size types had specific names, but those cast in different places often varied: see TYPE SIZES.

PONY SERVICE a brief summary of news obtained from a press association by wire, telephone, or mail, as by a small newspaper.

PORK 1. time copy. 2. copy saved over from one edition to be printed in a later edition.

POTBOILER something written for the immediate purpose of earning money quickly.

PRECEDE   1. a brief item printed, often in italics or bold-face, as at the beginning of a news story that has been set earlier, in order to give the latest developments or an editorial note.   2. a similar paragraph at the beginning of a story indicating that it is one in a series: opposite of FOLO (sense 3).

PREFACE   introductory or explanatory material written by an author, preceding his book: distinguished from FOREWORD, written by someone else. The preface usually tells subject, purpose, and plan of the book, and often contains acknowledgments of help received from others.

PRESS AGENT   a person whose work is getting publicity for an actor, institution, etc.

PRESS MARK   1. a design and/or inscription placed at the end of a book: the inscription gives certain publication data, as the printer's name, place and date of publication, etc.   2. a mark used to identify work done by a particular publisher: generally the same as COLOPHON, which see.

PRINTER   1. a person whose occupation is printing.   2. a teletype machine.   3. a device for making contact or projected prints from negatives.

PRINTER'S DEVIL★   an apprentice printer, or errand boy for a printer.

PRINTER'S MARK   a distinctive mark used to identify work done by a printer: at times it may merge with PRESS MARK, when the printer and publisher are the same.[46]

PRINTOUT   the output of a computer presented in type-written or printed form.

PRIVACY, RIGHT OF   the right of a citizen not to have details of his life explored in the press. By the nature of their chosen calling or activities, certain persons virtually forego this privilege; among them are politicians, actors, and criminals. The right of privacy also prevents the use of a person's name or picture in an advertisement without his permission.[47]

PRIVATE PRESS   a publisher of printed pieces, with the work done as an avocation or as a nonprofit endeavor. Editions are usually limited, and often numbered.

PRIVILEGED COMMUNICATION   1. an impartial report of legal or legislative proceedings: even if it contains false or defamatory material, it may not form the basis of a libel suit.   2. a communication that one may not be compelled to divulge, as from a patient to his doctor, or client to lawyer. The press continues to strive for court permission to refuse to divulge news sources.

PROCESS PRINTING   printing from three or four color plates to produce halftones with a range of color tones: see COLOR SEPARATION.

PROGRESSIVE PROOFS or PROGS   a set of proofs from the color plates for the parts of a picture to be printed in each of the three or four colors—yellow, red, blue, and sometimes black—used in process printing. Each color is shown alone and then in combination, in the order in which they are to be printed.

PROOF   1. a preliminary impression of set type produced on a hand press (*proof press*), to be checked against the original manuscript and marked for correction and changes by a proofreader, and sometimes the author. 2. such an impression of final copy to be used for reproduction. To *pull a proof* is to print such an impression.

PROOFREADER   a person who examines proof and marks it for corrections. See PROOFREADERS' MARKS (page 157).

PROPAGANDA   the dissemination of information, opinions, or ideas, especially in printed form, intended to support or discredit a nation, organization, etc. Now often suspected of being unduly slanted.

PUBLIC DOMAIN   the condition or status of material not protected by copyright or patent and thus available to the general public for use without fee.[48]

PUBLICIST   a press agent.

PUFF   a publicity release praising an individual, organization, etc., usually of little or no news value.

PULP MAGAZINES   magazines printed on cheap, bulky paper, and usually containing sensational stories.

PUT TO BED   1. to complete the operations preparatory to printing a newspaper: the paper is put to bed when the press is ready to start printing. The corresponding term for the magazine is *close*.   2. to continue working on a newspaper edition until the paper is ready to go to press.

Q-A a news story, magazine article, etc. that consists mostly of questions and answers, as an interview, or a recording of court procedures.

QU? Is this correct? A proofreader's mark, placed in the margin of proof as a query to editor or author.

QUAD or QUADRAT blank spacing material used to indent paragraphs and to space out at the ends of lines.

QUADDER a device on a linecaster that automatically spaces out centered material or automatically sets flush left or flush right.

QUARTO a book made up of leaves cut four from a sheet; eight pages, each measuring approximately 9½″ x 12″; 4to; 4°.[49]

QUERY 1. a question regarding accuracy of copy or proof from copy editor, proofreader, etc. 2. an inquiry from a news correspondent or free-lance writer to an editor outlining a story or article, and asking if it is wanted, and, if so, what length.

QUIRE 24 or 25 sheets of paper; one-twentieth of a ream.

QUOIN★ a notched metal, or sometimes wooden, wedge used to lock type elements securely in the chase, or to secure a block of type in the galley.

QUONKING noise, especially background chatter of an audience or studio workers, that interferes with the audio portion of a broadcast.

QUOTES 1. quoted material. 2. quotation marks.

RAG   a newspaper.

RAILROAD   to rush newspaper copy from the typewriter to the composing room without copy editing, or from the composing room to press without proofreading.

RAISED PRINTING   same as THERMOGRAPHY.

RATE CARD   a card issued periodically by a publication showing its advertising rates.

READABILITY   1. the qualities that make a piece of copy easy or difficult to read, considered editorially, as understanding of meaning. It can be measured by any of several methods or formulas that investigate various factors.[50] 2. legibility: in this sense, considered by many to be an inaccurate usage.

READERSHIP   1. the total number of readers of a publication, as distinguished from CIRCULATION.   2. a specific group of readers, often classified by age, sex, interests, etc. [*Seventeen* has a female *readership*].

READING NOTICE   an advertisement in a newspaper or magazine that is set in body type and in columns so as to appear the same as editorial matter. It is labeled "adv." at the end, usually inconspicuously.

READYPRINT   sections of newspapers bought already printed and ready to be incorporated into the rest of the paper, as comic or magazine sections.

REAM★   five hundred sheets of paper; twenty quires.

RECTO   a page on the right-hand side; the front of a leaf: it usually carries an odd number: opposed to VERSO.

REFERENCE MARK   any of a number of printing symbols, or superior numbers or letters, used to refer the reader to notes or other reference material.

REFERENCE MATTER   same as BACK MATTER.

REGISTER   the alignment of color plates in process printing: *register marks* are small crosses or other marks that are easily lined up to assure that the work is in register. In *overlap register,* the colors are intended to overlap each other; in *loose register,* exactness is not necessary to the total appearance of the print; in *hairline register,* the colors must meet with exact precision or the proper effect is lost.[51]

REGLET★   1. a thin strip of furniture, usually wooden but sometimes metal, for spacing out a form.   2. reglets collectively.

REJECTION SLIP   a printed card, letter or half-sheet sent by an editor to a free-lancer with his rejected manuscript, photographs, drawings, etc. Some of the kinder forms have a list with check-off squares to indicate the reason for rejection.

RELEASE COPY   copy sent or received in advance of its projected publication time or date, as wire service or agency features, a president's address, or an obit of a person expected to die shortly: sometimes shortened to *release:* also ADVANCE COPY.

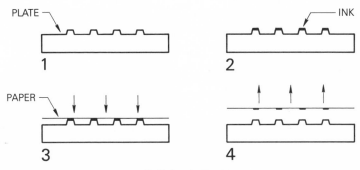

Relief printing

RELIEF a method of printing in which the image is carried on raised surfaces, as set type, halftone, etc.; letterpress: distinguished from INTAGLIO, LITHOGRAPHY.

REMARQUE a small design or scribble in the margin of an engraved plate to identify a stage of production: it appears only on proof (*remarque proof*).

REMOTE a broadcast originating outside the studio: also called NEMO.

REPORT 1. originally, gossip or rumors. 2. an account, as of an event, presented or procured for publication (hence, *reporter*). 3. in wire news service, all of the copy sent to a newspaper in a given day.[52]

REPRINT 1. a new printing of a book from the same type: see EDITION. 2. an article from a periodical printed separately and unbound, for special distribution.

REPRODUCTION PROOF a final proof printed with care, often on acetate or glossy paper, to be used as photographic copy for a printing plate: often shortened to *repro proof* or *repro*.

RESIST or ACID RESIST   a coating that does not allow the etching away of a portion of a photoengraving plate in the ACID BATH.

RESTRAINER   a chemical, usually potassium bromide, used to retard the action of a photographic developer.

RETRACTION   a correction of a false statement, usually printed in an equally prominent position. A retraction should not be printed merely to appease or as a matter of courtesy, but only if the copy was false; otherwise, it may be used as an admission in case of a suit for libel.

REUTERS NEWS AGENCY   British international news service.

REVERSE KICKER   see KICKER.

REVERSE TYPE   type that appears as white type on a black (or colored) background. A repro proof is pulled of type set in the ordinary way, and a line engraving is made of the solid color in the background.

REVISE   a proof taken after corrections have been made, used for further checking.

REWRITE MAN (or EDITOR)   a man in a newspaper office who writes up stories called in by legmen or reporters on beats, or rewrites publicity releases, wire news service material, etc.

RIBBON   1. a headline in smaller type under a banner. 2. a headline across the top of an inside page, or the front page of a second section.   3. the roll of perforated paper that guides the casting on a Monotype or automatic Linotype, or that activates the printing Justowriter.

RIM   the outer edge of the horseshoe-shaped copy desk. RIM MEN are the copyreaders who sit at the rim to do their work. See also SLOT.

RING   to draw a circle around; encircle, as to signify various directions in copy editing or proofreading. A ring around an abbreviation or figure indicates it should be spelled out; around a word indicates it should be abbreviated; also, ringing any punctuation mark means it should be a period.

RIVER   an irregular streak of white space extending down through several lines of set type, caused by wide spaces that happen to fall nearly under each other in successive lines: also called *gutter, channel, staircase.*

ROCK   to roughen the surface of a mezzotint plate with a *rocker* (also called *cradle*), as part of the preparation for printing.

ROCKET HEAD   a headline that uses the words of a news story set in boldface or display type.

ROMAN   a family of type divided into OLD-STYLE and MODERN, which see. Roman is the type most commonly used for body composition in printed matter. Each font of roman type ordinarily has a corresponding font of ITALIC.

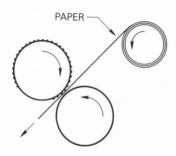

PAPER

Rotary press

ROTARY PRESS   a high-speed printing press with curved printing plates fitted onto revolving cylinders. The paper is fed from a continuous roll (WEB) between these plates and impression cylinders; used for long runs.

ROUGH   a preliminary layout or drawing, without details.

ROUNDUP   1. a news story or broadcast that has been compiled from several sources or geographic areas.   2. a brief broadcast of the latest news.

ROUT   to remove excess metal from the nonprinting areas of a printing plate by the use of a *router* or *routing machine*.

RUBBER CEMENT   an adhesive made of unvulcanized rubber in a chemical solvent, used in preparing artwork, dummies, etc.: it does not wrinkle paper as it dries, and is removable.

RUBY★   British name for *agate*, 5½-point type.

RULE   a strip of metal, usually brass, that is type-high, and used to print a line or lines, or to print boxes, etc.

RUN   a news reporter's beat.

RUNAROUND   printed matter that is arranged to fit around an illustration, often by being set in a narrow column.

RUN FLAT   do not change; use copy as it is: a direction to the printer, editor, etc.

RUN IN   a proofreader's or copy editor's instruction to the printer to print material without paragraphing.

RUNNING HEAD   1. the name of a book or chapter title printed at the head of each page: also *running title*. 2. the magazine title, date, etc. printed in the top margin on each page of some magazines. Similar material placed at the foot is called *running foot*. See also FOLIO (sense 7).

RUN OF PAPER, RUN-OF-PAPER   indicating that advertising may be placed wherever it is convenient to the publisher, or that color advertising may be placed anywhere, rather than being restricted to certain pages.

RUN OUT   1. a direction to the printer to make a hanging indention. 2. to fill out a line with leaders, quads, etc.

RUNOVER   1. same as OVERSET.   2. same as BREAK or BREAKOVER.

SACRED COW   a person, institution, etc. that receives favorable treatment in a particular publication or on a particular broadcasting station.

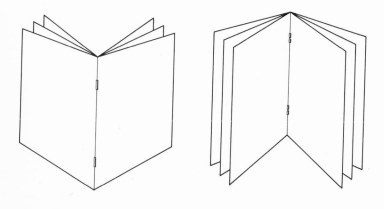

Saddle stitch

SADDLE STITCH   a binding stitch in which a wire staple is inserted through the center of the folded sheets from the back and clinched in the fold: see also SIDE STITCH.

SANS SERIF (FOLIO)

SANS SERIF   a class of type with uniform strokes and without serifs: also called BLOCK LETTERS. Gothic, Grotesque, and Futura are sans serif types.

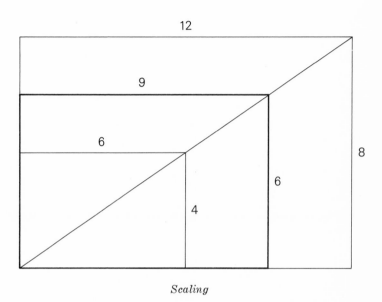

Scaling

SCALE   1. to calculate the correct relative dimensions of
   a photograph when it is to be reduced or enlarged.   2.
   this ratio as specified.

SCAN-A-GRAVER   a trademark for an electric engraving
   machine, by which a stylus acting on a plastic printing
   plate on a cylinder reproduces a halftone illustration
   that can be sent by wire: the stylus is controlled by an
   electric eye which scans the original and transmits electric impulses according to tone values.[53]

SCAREHEAD   a large, sensational headline, especially
   one that is likely to arouse fear.

SCHEDULE or SKED   1. the list of available stories made up each day by the editors of various departments of a newspaper.   2. a list of a day's assignments in a news office.   3. all the headlines used by a newspaper, as listed in an inventory: often called *hed sked*.   4. in wire news service, the list of stories scheduled to move on the wire during a given day.   5. the list of programs and announcements to be broadcast by a radio or television station during a day.

SCOOP   1. to get ahead of rival newspapers or reporters in covering and publishing a timely, sensational news story; beat.   2. such a news story; beat; exclusive.

SCORCHER   a device that dries a newly molded stereotype flong and curves it to fit the cylinder of a rotary press: also called *former, roaster*.

SCREAMER   1. an exceptionally large and bold banner, especially of a sensational nature.   2. an exclamation point: also sometimes called a *shriek*.

SCREEN   1. a glass plate or film ruled into minute squares that is interposed between the negative and plate in making a halftone from a continuous-tone original. The screen breaks the image into a DOT PATTERN that will reproduce tonal values.[54]   2. to photograph an illustration through such a screen.   3. a numerical designation of relative fineness of a screen or halftone, representing the number of dots per lineal inch, ranging ordinarily from 55 to 175. Rough papers such as newsprint take from 55- to 85-line screens; the smoother, coated papers used for offset allow 120-, 133-, or 150-line screens; the papers with a midrange of smoothness, such as those used for many magazines, use the midrange of halftone screens. Extremely glossy papers can take as fine a screen as 175- or 200-line.

SCRIPT   1. handwriting.   2. a typeface designed to resemble handwriting, with connecting letters: see also CURSIVE.   3. a copy of a play, radio or television show, motion picture, etc., with the directions for production included.

SECOND COMING TYPE   the largest, blackest headline type.

SECOND FRONT (PAGE)   the front page of a newspaper's second section: also called *split page.*

SEMIMONTHLY   a publication that appears twice a month: distinguished from BIMONTHLY.

SEMIWEEKLY   a publication that appears twice a week: distinguished from BIWEEKLY.

SERIF★   a tiny decorative finishing stroke at the end of a letter stroke: see BRACKETED SERIF, SQUARE SERIF, SANS SERIF.

SERIGRAPHY   silk screen printing as used in the fine arts.

SETOFF   same as OFFSET (sense 2).

SHANK   the body of a piece of type.

SHEET   1. a separate piece of paper fed into a press, as for printing a book: see entry for PAPER SIZES. Such a press is said to be *sheet-fed,* as opposed to *web-fed.*   2. a newspaper: often applied especially to a tabloid or other sensational newspaper [scandal *sheet*].[55]

SHEETWISE   indicating a method of imposition (*sheet imposition*) in which the front of a sheet or signature is printed from one form, and the back is printed from a different form: sometimes called WORK-AND-BACK: opposed to WORK-AND-TURN or WORK-AND-TUMBLE, in which both sides are printed from the same form.

SHELFBACK   see BACKBONE (sense 1).

SHELTER BOOKS (or MAGAZINES)   magazines that concentrate on housing or home decoration.

SHIRTTAIL   a short related news item added in a paragraph at the end of a news article.

SHORT AND   the ampersand (&).

SHORTS   pages needed to fill out an incomplete edition.

SHORTSTOP   a rinse in a weak acetic acid solution between the photographic developer and the FIXING BATH, to stop the action of the developer: also called *stop bath.*

SHOULDER   the nonprinting plane surface of type from which the raised character projects. The shoulder may include leading, usually two points: 10/12 type is 10-point type on a 12-point body. The portions of the shoulder between the strokes, or immediately adjacent to the projecting character, are called the *counter*. See illustration for TYPE.

SHOUT   an exclamation point.

SIDEBAR   a feature presented as a companion to a straight news report, giving sidelights on human-interest aspects, sometimes elucidating just one aspect of the story.

SIDE HEAD   a heading set flush left.

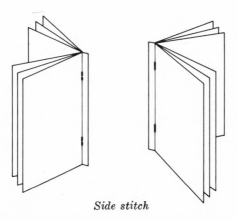

Side stitch

SIDE STITCH   a binding stitch in which wire staples or thread is stitched through folded signatures, gathered together, about ⅛″ from the folded edge.

SIGMA DELTA CHI   journalism fraternity, founded in 1909.

SIGNATURE   1. the folded pages of copy printed on one sheet of paper in a single imposition: signatures are commonly in multiples of 16.   2. a number or letter in the corner of the first page of each signature, indicating the order in which the signatures are to be bound into the completed volume: contrasted with *collating marks*.

SILHOUETTE   a halftone plate or print in which only the image is printed; the background is completely cut or etched away.

SILK SCREEN   a printing process utilizing the stencil principle, in which paint or ink is forced through raw silk (stretched on a frame) by a squeegee in areas not covered by an impermeable substance, onto paper or other surface.[56]

SILLY SEASON   a period when news is slow, as late summer, and news reporters resort to trivialities to fill up the paper.[57]

SILVER PRINT   1. an offset page proof.   2. a photographic print that has been used as the basis for a pen and ink drawing directly on the print, after which the photographic image is bleached out, leaving the line drawing for engraving.

SINKAGE   the distance the text is dropped down on the beginning page of a chapter, from the usual top line of a page.

SKED   schedule.

SKYLINE   1. a banner head set above the nameplate on a newspaper front page: also *over-title*.   2. a kicker or teaser set over a main headline, especially one that is underlined.

SLANT   1. a particular point of view from which a news story, article, etc. is written in order to appeal to a specific audience, to sell to a specific publication, or to favor a bias on the part of the publication or writer.   2. to write a story from a certain point of view.

SLICK   a high-circulation consumer magazine printed on glossy, coated stock, with illustrated stories or articles of popular appeal; glossy.

SLIPSHEET   a sheet of paper or cardboard placed between printed sheets as they come off the press, to prevent offset.

SLOT   the middle of the horseshoe-shaped copy desk where the news editor or copy editor (sometimes called *slotman*) sits. To be *in the slot* is to be in charge of the copy desk. The outer edge is the RIM.

SLUG   1. a line of type cast in one piece from a linecaster. 2. a thick lead, commonly six points, used for spacing. 3. an identifying word or phrase used by a reporter or wire service editor at the top of each section of copy having to do with a particular story; all copy carries the slug until the story is complete or the paper is finally put together: also called *slugline, catchline, guide, guideline*. 4.(a) to insert a slug (lead) between lines of type. (b) to put a slug (catchline) on copy.

SLUSH   1. material sent into a publication, especially a magazine, by free-lancers: the collective term for unsolicited manuscripts is *slushpile*.   2. cheaply sentimental copy; trash; drivel.

SMALL CAPITALS   capital letters of a smaller size than regular capitals: they are traditionally the X-HEIGHT of letters of the font to which they belong, but sometimes vary.

SMASHING   the process of compressing the sewn signatures of a book to a uniform bulk, with a heavy, rapid squeeze by means of a press (*smasher* or *smashing machine*), so that it will be flat for binding: the back is given a preliminary compression (*nipping*) as it goes through the *nipper*.

SOB SISTER   a newspaperwoman (sometimes said also of a man) who writes foolishly sentimental or pathetic news stories. An outdated term.

SOC (säk)   the society (or women's) section of a newspaper.

SOLID   designating type matter set without leading between the lines.

SORTS   all of the types in a job case. When all of the types in a section have been used, the compartment is "out of sorts." To "pick for sorts" is to pick individual type characters out of standing matter to use on another job. They are temporarily replaced by types inserted with the feet up.

SOUP   photographic developer.

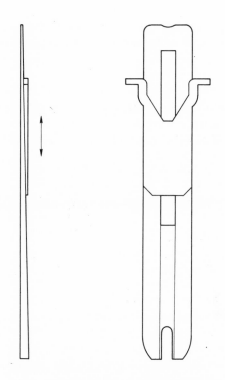

Spaceband (*linecaster*)

SPACEBAND a wedge-shaped metal device that automatically expands as needed to provide proper spacing
between matrices in a line of type produced on a linecasting machine.

SPIKE to reject copy: from editors' practice of impaling
rejected copy on a spindle file.

SPINE see BACKBONE (sense 1).

SPLIT PAGE   the front page of a newspaper's second section; second front page.

SPLIT RUN   a press run in which two or more portions of an issue of a newspaper or periodical contain copy, advertising, etc. differing from that in the other portion or portions. Used to test appeal of an advertisement, or to present local copy for different geographical sections.

SPOT NEWS   current news; news reported immediately, or live from the scene.

SPOTTING UP   the process of pasting patches of tissue (OVERLAYS) on or under the tympan during makeready.

SPREAD   1. a news story or feature, often with illustrations, that occupies more than one column, and may extend to a full page or several pages.   2. same as DOUBLE SPREAD.

SQUABBLE   to disarrange type that has been set so that it is awry.

L   SQUARE SERIF (MEMPHIS)

SQUARE SERIF   a class of type in which the serifs are the same weight as the monotonal main strokes: also known as *block serif* and *Egyptian,* and in England as *slab bracketed* (type). Cairo, Karnak, and Memphis are square serif types.

SQUIB   1. a brief, comparatively unimportant news item, sometimes used merely as a filler.   2. a lampoon.

STABLE   collectively, all of the authors whose work is published by one publishing house or publication.

STAFFER   a writer who is a member of a newspaper or magazine staff, as opposed to a STRINGER or other correspondent.

STAGE   to prevent further etching of acid in certain portions of a plate by coating with a resist; stop out.

STANDARD RATE AND DATA SERVICE   an organization that issues a number of publications giving advertising rates and other data for consumer magazines, business publications, newspapers, radio, television, transportation advertising, etc.

STANDING MATTER (or TYPE)   type that is kept set in order to use at a later time, or kept set permanently because it is used often, as column headings, etc. Also called PICKUP.

STARCH ADVERTISEMENT READERSHIP SERVICE   a research organization for measuring and evaluating the readership and effectiveness of advertisements in publications.

STEM   1. any of the main or heavy strokes of a letter, especially those letters that have a bar (T), crossbar (A,H,), bowl (b,q,), or shorter, oblique lines (k,y).   2. the body of a piece of type: this term is not as often used as *body* or *shank*.

STEREOTYPE   1. a duplicate printing plate, for high-speed long runs, cast in one piece from a papier-mâché matrix (FLONG) that has been molded from a page of set type or other printing elements: often shortened to *stereo*.   2. to cast such a printing plate.   3. a cliché.

STET★   let it stand: used to mark portions of copy about which the printer may have doubt, as copy that was previously changed, or marked for deletion. In addition to the word *stet* (written in the margin by proofreaders, circled in the copy or margin by copy editors), a word or phrase is sometimes underlined with a row of dots (*stet marks*).

STICK   1. a composing stick.   2. the galley of a linecaster that receives the completed slug.   3. a small amount of copy, usually about 150 words: a *stickful* occupies about two inches of space in a newspaper column.

STONE   see IMPOSING STONE.

STOP   1. a punctuation mark, especially a period.   2. the aperture of a camera lens, usually adjustable.   3. the number (*F-number*) used to designate a particular adjustment of the camera lens.

STOP BATH   same as SHORTSTOP.

STOP OUT   1. to prevent an acid bite from proceeding in a given section of an engraving or etching by coating with an acid resist, as dragon's blood; to stage.   2. to interpose something opaque between a negative and certain portions of a developing print to prevent further action of light.   3. to coat certain portions of an electrotype with wax to prevent the deposit of metal and preserve a blank area.

STOW   1. a direction to the printer: it is typed as a slugline on features, fillers, etc. that will not be changed. 2. to put a feature or story on a page that is made up early in the newspaper day.

STRAIGHT 1. designating type matter that is simple body composition, without display type, tables, variations, etc. 2. designating news that is written as a simple presentation of facts.

STREAMER same as BANNER.

STRINGER★ 1. a local part-time newspaper reporter, sometimes one who works for more than one publication. 2. a newspaper or magazine correspondent from an outlying or faraway area who sends in copy irregularly, often features, background analysis, or depth reporting: originally called *string correspondent*.

STRIPPING 1. the combining of two or more negatives for platemaking (for photoengraving or photolithography) by removing the image emulsions from the film base and putting them in proper position on a glass plate to form a FLAT: done by a *stripper*. 2. the removing of an electrotype shell from the mold.

STROBE an electronic photo flash unit with an extremely brilliant, high-speed flash. It is battery-operated or may be plugged in, and used repeatedly. May also have separate units (*slaves*) that are set off instantly by action of the light when the primary strobe flashes.

STUDHORSE TYPE the blackest and biggest headline type.

STYLE a specified manner of dealing with punctuation, capitalization, spellings, etc., as by a particular publisher.

STYLEBOOK a book that sets forth prescriptive rules for style.

SUBHEAD   a boldface subordinate heading, often flush left, used to mark off the divisions of a subject, or simply to break up a long stretch of body type.

SUBSTANCE   same as BASIS WEIGHT.

SUPER   1. short for *supersized and calendered* (S.S.& C.) : a smooth-surface book paper that has been sized and calendered.   2. a loose, open-weave cotton material used as reinforcement for the binding of a book: also called *crash,* or in England, *mull.*

SUPERIOR   designating letters or figures smaller than the type used, that appear above the line of type[156]: also called *superscripts.*

SUPPLEMENT   material added at the end of a book, necessary to its completeness. It may be quite extensive, and is usually matter that has become available after the main body of the book has been set into type: distinguished from APPENDIX and ADDENDUM.

SWASH LETTERS   capital letters in some italics (as Garamond or Caslon) that end in long, sweeping, flourishing lines.

SWEATING   the mounting of a photoengraving or electrotype to a base by soldering.

TABLOID★   a newspaper with pages about half the size of a regular newspaper, characterized by much pictorial matter, large, often sensational headlines, and concise reporting. Often shortened to *tab.*

TABOO   designating words, phrases, subjects, etc. not permitted in a given publication.

TACK   the degree of stickiness of ink, glue, etc. that is not yet dry.

TAG   a closing; something at the end, as (a) the symbol -30-, -END-, etc. printed at the end of a story, or a notice that there will be another feature in the series, (b) an announcement at the end of a program or commercial: a *live tag* is a local announcement at the end of a recorded or taped commercial or program, (c) a cliché, especially one used as a final phrase, intended to be a clincher: also *tag line*.

TAIL   1. the bottom of a printed page.   2. the end of a chapter or book.   3. the descenders of letters such as g, y, and Q.

TAILPIECE   a small type decoration or drawing at the end of a story or chapter, or at the bottom of a single printed page.

TAKE   the portion of copy being handled by a typesetter at one time, especially a small part of a long newspaper or wire service story: to *rush copy in short takes* is to bring copy continuously in order to speed up printing.[58]

TASS   the Russian state-owned news agency.

TEAR SHEET 1. a sheet torn from a publication, as to send to an advertiser so he can see his printed advertisement. 2. a sheet from a publication printed separately, and unbound, to be distributed or sold for a special purpose: also called REPRINT, especially if the sheet is folded over as a leaflet.

TEASER a short line set in smaller type above a headline; kicker.

TELEPHOTO a trademark for a method of transmitting photographs by wire, or a picture so transmitted.

TELETYPESETTER a trademark for 1. an apparatus that perforates tape upon typing on a keyboard. 2. an attachment that automatically operates a linecasting machine from perforated tape. 3. a wire service circuit on which justified copy is transmitted. It also produces a perforated tape to be fed into automatic linecasters.

TEXT 1. black letter type. 2. the main body of a book or other printed work. 3. body type, as distinguished from headings, display type, etc. 4. type matter, as distinguished from illustrations. 5. a kind of paper with a somewhat rough finish, used for booklets, programs, etc.

THERMOGRAPHY a process that simulates embossing; used on stationery, cards, etc. The freshly inked letterpress letters are dusted with a resinous powder and exposed to heat, which makes the letters rise as though embossed. Also called *raised printing*.

THETA SIGMA PHI society for women in journalism and communications, founded in 1909.

THINK PIECE   a feature presenting news analysis, background material, personal opinion, etc., sometimes as a sidebar to a straight news story.

THIRTY★ or -30-   word or symbol used to mark the end of a story. The symbol # is sometimes used on copy, as is -END-. Any of these conventions is sometimes called the *tag*.

THUMBNAIL   1. a small rough sketch; a miniature layout.   2. a picture, usually of a person, that takes up less than a full column (usually half a column), as in a newspaper.[59]   3. a very short literary sketch.

TICKLE   to make note of a news item that might make good copy some time in the future because of further developments that are expected. The file or book for such notes is a *tickler*.

TIED LETTERS   ligatures.

TIGHT   1. designating a newspaper that has little room for news because there is a great deal of advertising: opposite of OPEN.   2. designating a newspaper on a day when there are a great many newsworthy events to record, and hardly enough space to cover them all.

TIME COPY   1. copy that may be held over and printed later if space does not permit immediate publication. 2. copy set into type and held for later publication.

TINT BLOCK   a solid or screened plate used to reproduce color: it is often used under pictures or as background for overprinted type matter. When the plate is screened, the tone value is lightened.[60]

TIP   to paste an inserted page, as an illustration or end papers, into a book by putting ⅛″ paste along the gutter edge.

TOENAIL   1. a quotation mark.   2. a parenthesis: sometimes *fingernail*.

TOMBSTONES   headlines of the same size, usually boldface, placed side by side.

TRADE BOOK   a book intended for sale through regular trade channels, as distinguished from textbooks, some reference books, or those sold through book clubs, organizations, etc.

TRADE JOURNAL   a magazine whose intended audience is a specified trade or business.

TRAMP PRINTER   an independent printer who works in one shop, then another, and never stays in one shop long: a derogatory term.

TRANSITIONAL   designating a roman type having some characteristics of both Modern and Old Style: Cheltenham is an example.

TRANSPOSE   1. to exchange positions of letters, words, groups of words, or lines, by typographical error, etc. (*transposition*).   2. to correct such errors.

TURN   copy "turns" when it appears in several columns, as a story on a page, or under a picture, box, etc., or when it runs from one page to the next.

TURNED RULE or SORT   a rule or type character (sort) turned with its broad or feet side up so that a black oblong or square prints, within a block of copy, indicating alterations or additions are to come.

TURN STORY   the story that continues from the last column of one page (the *turn column*) to the first column of the next, thus requiring no jump head.

TUSCHE★   a greasy black liquid used for drawing or painting on a lithographic plate, as a resist in etching, or to stop out nonprinting areas in silk screen printing.

TYMPAN   sturdy paper or parchment that covers the packing on the platen or impression cylinder: also *tympan sheet.*

TYPE★   1. a metal, or sometimes wood, printing element with a raised character on a rectangular body, used in relief printing.   2. such pieces collectively.   3. a printed character or characters; printed matter.

TYPE CLASSIFICATION   the major classes of type are roman, text, square serif, sans serif, and novelty (or ornamental).[61] In descending order, type is further classified by FAMILY, SERIES, and FONT.

TYPE-HIGH   the height of a piece of type, linecaster slug, or other printing element from feet to printing surface: in the United States and Great Britain, standardized at .9186 in.

TYPE LOUSE   a bug searched for by apprentice printers at the direction of their co-workers, between the characters of set type when it has been sloshed with cleaning fluid: when the type is quickly pushed together, the "lice," in the form of drops of inky fluid, are on the printer's devil's face.

TYPE METAL   an alloy of tin, antimony, and lead.

TYPESETTER   1. a compositor.   2. a machine for setting type; typesetting machine.

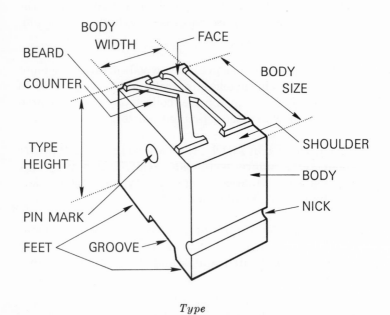

Type

TYPE SIZES Originally, each size of type was known by an individual name, but the sizes cast by different foundries varied slightly. A uniform system of measurement, based on the point system was adopted in 1878: see POINT SYSTEM. Many names of the most common sizes of type have carried over to the point size of type that is its nearest equivalent. Many books, therefore, designate a type name as the "old" name, with the understanding that the "new" name is simply the nearest size of type in points.

The sizes differ from one another by half points from 3 point to 7, by single points from 7 to 12, and usually by two points from 12 to 24. Sizes larger than this are in even numbers.

A type size designates the body size of the type, not the size of its face. Thus different families of type that are the same size can, and do, vary greatly in the size of the x-height and width, and therefore vary in size of the over-all letters as seen by the eye.[62]

TYPO typographical error.

TYPOGRAPHY 1. the art or process of setting and arranging type. 2. the process of printing from composed type; letterpress printing. 3. the appearance, arrangement, or style of printed matter. 4. loosely, and inaccurately, book design.

UNDERLAY a patch or sheet of paper, from tissue to cardboard, laid or pasted under type or a printing plate during makeready to help insure a uniform impression.

UNDERLINES 1. a caption; legend. 2. horizontal lines under lines of written or type matter, especially under typed words to indicate they are to be set in italics.

UNITED PRESS a news service founded in 1882, merged with International News Service in 1958 to form United Press International. Wire service commenced in 1915.

UNITED PRESS INTERNATIONAL a privately owned international wire news service that provides news copy, features, news analyses, and photographs to subscriber newspapers, radio and television stations: it was formed in 1958 by a merger of United Press and International News Service, has over 7,000 subscribers, and was the first news service to prepare copy especially for radio, in 1935.[63]

UPPER CASE the capital letters in a font, formerly kept in the upper of two type cases facing the compositor: distinguished from LOWER CASE, the small letters.

UP STYLE indicating printed matter that is styled with more words capitalized than usual: ordinarily the author's choice of up or down style is respected.

VANITY PRESS a publisher who puts out work paid for by the authors themselves.

VARITYPER a trademark for a typewriter that justifies lines, and has interchangeable type faces.

VERSO   a page on the left-hand side; back of a leaf: it usually carries an even number: opposed to RECTO.

VIDEO   the picture part of a television broadcast.

VIGNETTE   1. an ornamental border of vine leaves, grapes, etc. used for page decoration.   2. a halftone or photograph that gradually fades into the background at the edges, without a discernible borderline.   3. a newspaper nameplate: used thus by the San Francisco *Chronicle*.   4. a very short sketch or story.

VISUAL   a rough layout.

WASH DRAWING   a water color done in shades of black and gray, often intended for halftone reproduction.

WATER HAUL   fruitless research, interviewing, writing, or other work on a feature or story.

WEB   a continuous roll of paper fed into, and woven over and under the cylinders of a high-speed rotary press, as for printing newspapers[64]: such a press is said to be *web-fed*, as opposed to *sheet-fed*.

WHITE SPACE   the blank areas surrounding or between blocks of type, illustrations, or other printing elements on the printed page.

WIDOW   a short line of type at the end of a paragraph. If it carries over to the top of a new column or page, the writer or editor often rewrites the copy to eliminate the widow. Some typographers consider a line to be a widow if it is shorter than a quarter of a line. One word or part of a word is recognized as such in any kind of copy editing. Special pains are taken to eliminate widows in picture captions.

WIRE FILER   in wire news service, the newsman who decides where each story will move and when.

WIREPHOTO   a trademark for a process of transmitting pictures by wire; also, a picture transmitted in this way.

WIRE SIDE   the side of paper next to the wire in manufacturing; the wrong side: opposite of FELT SIDE.

WOLFF'S TELEGRAPHEN AGENCY   wire news service in Germany.

WOODCUT   an engraving on a block of wood, type-high, for relief printing.

WOODEN HEAD   uninteresting headline.

WORK-AND-BACK   a method of printing in which one side of a signature is printed from one form, and the other side is printed from a different form.

WORK-AND-TUMBLE   a method of printing in which both sides of a signature are printed from the same form, the paper is turned to be fed to a different gripper edge, and printed on the reverse side. Both sides of two pieces are thus printed.

WORK-AND-TURN   a method of printing in which both sides of a signature are printed from the same form, the paper is turned to be fed to the same gripper edge, and printed on the reverse side. Both sides of two pieces are thus printed.

WORKER (PLATE)   an electrotype plate used for printing: distinguished from CASTER.

WORK-UP   an ink mark made by spacing material that rises in the form and prints on the sheet.

WOVE PAPER   paper having the appearance of a piece of tightly woven cloth, made on a tight screen.

WRAPAROUND   a four-page book section, as an insert, that is folded, placed on the outside of a signature, and sewed along with it: also called *wrap*.

WRAPUP or WRAP-UP   1. a complete news story, as put together from several takes.   2. in wire news service, a final, complete write-up on a story that has had several leads: also called a *write-through lead*. It is more complete, and contains more detail, than a summary.   3. in newscasting, a final presentation of the major news stories of a specified period, usually a day.

WRITE-UP   a news story or feature, magazine article, etc.

WRONG FONT   a type character of a different typeface or size than the rest of the material being set, or different from that specified to be set in a certain place.

XEROGRAPHY★ the process of making small lithographic plates or duplicate paper copies by the use of
static electricity: a negatively charged powder fixes the
image.

Printing ↕ X-HEIGHT

X-HEIGHT the dimension of type from top to bottom
without descenders or ascenders; height of the lower-
case x.

XYLOGRAPH a woodcut, or a print made from this: the
art of cutting or printing these is *xylography*. An old
term.

YELLOW JOURNALISM★ cheaply sensational journalism, with large black headlines, highly emotional and
often risqué human-interest copy, and gory pictures.

ZINC ETCHING a low-cost relief printing plate of a
line drawing; zinc line cut.

ZINC WHITE same as CHINESE WHITE.

ZIP-A-TONE a trademark for plastic sheets that carry
a variety of regular patterns, affixed by the artist to fill
in areas in artwork, to be made into line cuts: compare
with BENDAY.

III. Abbreviations

AA, A.A. author's alteration: see ALTERATION

AAAA American Association of Advertising Agencies: also *4A*

AAEA American Agricultural Editors' Association

AAIE American Association of Industrial Editors

AASDJ American Association of Schools and Departments of Journalism

A.A.W. Advertising Association of the West

ABC Audit Bureau of Circulations

ABP American Business Press, Inc.

ACEJ American Council on Education for Journalism: the group responsible for the accreditation of schools and departments of journalism

ACP Associated Church Press; Associated Construction Publications

advt. (plural advts.) advertisement(s)

AEJ Association for Education in Journalism

AFTRA American Federation of Television and Radio Artists

ag bf, ag. b.f. agate boldface

AIGA American Institute of Graphic Arts

AJPA   American Jewish Press Association

ALA   Authors League of America

ALMA   Association of Literary Magazines of America

A.M.   a morning paper

ANA   Association of National Advertisers

ANG, A.N.G.   American Newspaper Guild

ANPA, A.N.P.A.   American Newspaper Publishers Association

a.p.   author's proof

AP, A.P.   Associated Press

A.P.A.   Agricultural Publishers Association

APP   Associated Purchasing Publications

APPM   Association of Publication Production Managers

ASBPE   American Society of Business Press Editors

ASCAP   American Society of Composers, Authors and Publishers

ASJSA   American Society of Journalism School Administrators

ASME   American Society of Magazine Editors

ASMP   American Society of Magazine Photographers;
Association of Screen Magazine Publishers

ASNE   American Society of Newspaper Editors

bf, b.f.   boldface

B.J.   Bachelor of Journalism

bklr.   black letter

BOM, B.O.M.   Business Office Must: copy that must be
printed, regardless of space considerations

BPA, B.P.A.   Business Publications Audit

brev.   brevier

c. and s.c.   caps and small caps

cap(s)   capital letter(s)

C.C.A.   Controlled Circulation Audit

col.   column

comp.   comprehensive; composition; compositor

CPA   Catholic Press Association

cpl   characters per line

CQ   correct; all right: a mark put on copy to indicate that the spelling of a name or the like is correct

CX   correct copy: a direction to the printer

DA, D.A.   Dictionary of Americanisms

dj, d.j.   dust jacket

D.M.A.A.   Direct Mail Advertising Association

do.   *ditto* [L.] the same

doc., docu.   document

dt.   date

dwg.   drawing

E. & P.   *Editor & Publisher* magazine

ed.   edited; edition; editor

edit.   edited; edition

E.F.   English finish (paper)

EPA   Evangelical Press Association

EPAA   Educational Press Association of America

f., ff.   (and) following page(s)

f., f°   folio

F & G's   folded and gathered signatures

F.C.   follow copy: an instruction to the printer: "even if it goes out the window" is the classic addition for emphasis

FCC   Federal Communications Commission

fol.   folio; following

f.v.   *folio verso* [L.] on the back of the page

FYI   for your information

g.e.   gilt edges (bookbinding)

Goth., goth.   Gothic

GPO   Government Printing Office

HFR   hold for release

HI, H.I.   human interest

HTK   hed to kum (head to come): marked on copy sent ahead of its headline

ICIE   International Council of Industrial Editors

ID   identification

IFCJ   International Federation of Catholic Journalists

IFPP   International Federation of the Periodical Press

imp.   *imprimatur* [L.] let it be printed

INP   International News Photo

INS   International News Service: see UNITED PRESS IN-
TERNATIONAL

IPI   International Press Institute

ital, itax   italics

ITU   International Telecommunication Union; International Typographical Union

IUAJ   International Union of Agricultural Journalists

JO   journalist (military)

JPS   Jewish Publication Society of America

JQ   *Journalism Quarterly*

lc, l.c.   lower case

lca   lower case alphabet

ld   lead

lf, l.f.   lightface

l.o.   layout

MAB, M.A.B.   Magazine Advertising Bureau, Inc.

m.e.   marbled edges (bookbinding)

M.E.   managing editor

M.F.   machine finish (paper)

MPA, M.P.A.   Magazine Publishers Association; Methodist Press Association

MR   motivational research

MS, ms (plural MSS, mss)   manuscript(s)

N.A.M.P.   National Association of Magazine Publishers

NANA   North American Newspaper Alliance, Inc.

NARTB   National Association of Radio and Television Broadcasters

NASW   National Association of Science Writers

NCS   National Cartoonists Society

n.d., ND   no date

NE   new edition

NEA, N.E.A.   National Editorial Association; Newspaper Enterprise Association, Inc.

NFPW   National Federation of Press Women

N.I.A.A.   National Industrial Advertisers Association

n.l.   new line

NNS   National Newspaper Syndicate

N.O.A.B.   National Outdoor Advertising Bureau

n.p.   no place

O.A.A.A.   Outdoor Advertising Association of America

OP   out of print; title discontinued (book publishing)

OPC   Overseas Press Club

op. ed.   opposite the editorial page

p., pg.   page

P.D.   public domain

PE, P.E.   printer's error

P.I.B.   Publishers Information Bureau, Inc.

PIO   Public Information Officer (military)

P.M.   an afternoon newspaper

PNS   Publishers Newspaper Syndicate

POQ   *Public Opinion Quarterly*

pp.   pages; privately printed

PR, P.R.   ·public relations; press release

PRO   Public Relations Officer (military)

PU, P.U.   pick up: direction to the printer, wire news editor, etc.

pub., publ.   published; publisher; publishing

PW   *Publisher's Weekly*

r., ro.   recto

RH   relative humidity (papermaking)

RNA   Religious Newswriters Association

RNS   Religious News Service

rom   roman

ROP, R.O.P.   run of paper

RP   reprint; reprinting

S. & S.C.   sized and supercalendered (paper)

SBME   Society of Business Magazine Editors

SBPA   Southern Baptist Press Association

s.c.   single column; small caps; supercalendered (paper)

SDX   Sigma Delta Chi

sm. c., sm. caps   small capitals

SMW   Society of Magazine Writers

S.N.P.A.   Southern Newspaper Publishers Association

SRDS, S.R.D.S.   Standard Rate and Data Service

SS, S.S.   same size (photography)

S.S.& C.   supersized and calendered (paper)

STWP   Society of Technical Writers and Publishers

TBA, T.B.A.   to be announced

t.f.   till forbid: an order accompanying advertising, indicating that it should be printed or broadcast as given until further notice: also *T.F.N.* till further notice

TK   to come: marked on copy to indicate something more is to come

TNX   thanks; thank you

TOC   Table of Contents

TOP   temporarily out of print

tr.   translated; translation; translator; transpose

TSP   Theta Sigma Phi

TTS   teletypesetter

TY   thank you

u. and l.c.   upper and lower case

uc, u.c.   upper case

UP, U.P.   United Press: see UNITED PRESS INTERNATIONAL

UPI, U.P.I.   United Press International

UPIN   United Press International Newsfeatures

unp   unpaged

USIA   United States Information Agency

v., vo.   verso

vs.   verse; versus

WC   with corrections: a direction to the printer that corrections need to be made on proof before printing

wf, w.f.   wrong font

WNS   Women's News Service

WSBP   Western Society of Business Publications

Proofreaders' Marks

⊲	Delete	⊙	Period
◡	Close up	⋟	Comma
⊚	Delete and close up	⊙	Colon
#	Space or more space	⋏	Semicolon
Eq. #	Equalize ⌄space⌃between ⌄words	/?	Question mark
▢	Indent 1 em	(?)	Query to author
ld	Insert lead between lines	/!	Exclamation point
⊲ *ld*	Take out lead	/=/	Hyphen
⊥	Push down lead that prints	⟨/⟩	Parentheses
⟲	Reverse; turn over	[/]	Brackets
¶	Begin a paragraph	ⱱ	Quotation marks; "quotes"
⊗	Broken letter	ⱱ	Apostrophe or 'single quote'
wf	Wrong font	⊤ᴍ	Em dash
⌉	Move to right	⊤ɴ	En dash
⌊	Move to left	ⱱ	Superscript
⌉⌊	Center	⟨	Subscript
⊔	Lower letters or words	*lig*	Use ligature fi
⊓	Raise letters or words	*lf*	Lightface type
═	Straighten line	*bf*	Boldface type
‖	Align type vertically	*rom*	Roman type
⋀	Insert matter from margin	*ital*	Italic type
tr	Transpose letters words or	*cap*	Capitals
⟨sp⟩	Spell out	*s.c.*	Small capitals
stet	Let it stand—all matter above dots	*lc*	Lower-case Letter

Sample Copy

The process of acquiring a college education is an arduous voyage on an immense sea of knowledge in what the student often suspects is a ~~confoundedly~~ inadequate craft. He has various captains to gide him in fishing for the tastiest morsels at different hours of the day, and each thinks species of facts and fancies are of far more value than what the student may catch under the direction of his next hour's captain. The pressure to learn a great deal very fast is constant. The student says a thousand time, "I will go back and read more about that when I have time, but he must move on to new pursuits, and he never go can back. No sooner does he learn to hold a gaff or even find out what a gaff is), when it seems he is expected to catch Moby Dick.

Now and then the scholar comes into port to unload his latest catch for evaluation. If the haul weighs light, he must redouble his efforts. story weather, doldrums, and mal de mer must be ignored or overcome.

Yet graduation day does arrive. The graduat is truly educated if he realizes on that day that he has gathered only small fry from the top of an abundant ocean and that the completion of his 4-year voyage calls not for pride but for humility for only now, as he turns toward land, is he aware that he has drawn but little from the depths.

The process of acquiring a college education is an arduous voyage on an immense sea of knowledge in what the student often suspects is a confoundedly inadequate craft. He has various captains at different hours of the day to guide him in fishing for the tastiest morsels, and each thinks his species of facts and fancies are of far more value than what the student may catch under the direction of his next hour's captain.

The pressure to learn a great deal very fast is constant. The student says a thousand times, "I will go back and read more about that when I have time," but he must move on to new pursuits, and he never can go back. No sooner does he learn to hold a gaff (or even find out what a gaff is), when it seems he is expected to catch Moby Dick.

Now and then the scholar comes into port to unload his latest catch for evaluation. If the haul weighs light, he must redouble his efforts. Stormy weather, doldrums, and *mal de mer* must be ignored or overcome.

Yet graduation day does arrive. The graduate is truly educated if he realizes on that day that he has gathered only small fry from the top of an abundant ocean; and that the completion of his four-year voyage calls not for pride, but for humility—for only now, as he turns toward land, is he aware that he has drawn but little from the depths.

Notes

CHAPTER I

1. Frank James Price, "Journalism Enrollments Hit New High at 24,445," *Journalism Quarterly*, XLIV (Winter, 1967), 812.

2. William L. Rivers, *The Mass Media* (New York: Harper and Row, Publishers, 1964), p. 10.

3. This intelligence from Harold Kent, Jr. of the San Francisco Bureau of United Press International, who often hears on a morning radio newscast the copy virtually as he has prepared it during the lobster trick.

4. Curtis D. MacDougall, *Interpretative Reporting* (New York: The Macmillan Company, 1963), p. 6.

5. *World Almanac*, 1968, p. 162.

6. *The Cleveland Press*, February 24, 1969, p. 46.

7. MacDougall, *op. cit.*

8. Wesley C. Clark, "The Future of Mass Communications," *Journalism Tomorrow*, ed. Wesley C. Clark (Syracuse: Syracuse University Press, 1958), p. 8.

9. The issue of January 21, 1968.

10. The issue of April 3, 1969.

11. The journalism terms discussed in this section are printed in all capitals for easy reference.

12. The date 1907 is agreed upon in Merriam-Webster's *Third Edition* and Jacobi's glossary in Roland E. Wolseley, *Understanding Magazines* (Ames, Iowa: The Iowa State University Press, 1965). This date is also given by H. L. Mencken, *The American Language*, Suppl. I (New York: Alfred A. Knopf, Inc., 1945), p. 329, n. 6, with a tale about Burgess' first use of the word. But Mencken also mentions that Burgess "launched" the word in *Burgess Unabridged* in 1914, which would account for the appearance of this date in *Webster's New World Dictionary* and Wentworth and Flexner's *Dictionary of American Slang*.

13. At least this is the explanation in the *Century Dictionary*. The *Oxford English Dictionary* says, "As to the origin . . . nothing has been ascertained. . . ." OED's first

date is 1779. No attempt is made to explain its origin in the other general dictionaries, nor the printing sources.

14. Robert E. Parks, "The Natural History of the Newspaper," *Mass Communications,* ed. Wilbur Schramm (Urbana, Illinois: University of Illinois Press, 1960), p. 10.

The *Oxford English Dictionary* agrees that *Fourth Estate* was used to mean "the mob" in earlier times. Its first citation for the term is in this sense, from Fielding in 1752.

15. Edward Carpenter, ed., *A House of Kings* (New York: The John Day Company, 1966), p. 90.

16. Vol. V, p. 238.

17. Within the entry for *Caxton,* p. 366.

18. Mencken, Suppl. I, p. 328, n. 8.

19. Frank Luther Mott, "The War of the Sunday Papers: Yellow Journalism" *American Journalism: A History: 1690–1960* (3rd ed.; New York: The Macmillan Company, 1963), pp. 524–26.

20. Roosevelt's speech is printed in full in *The Muckrakers,* ed. Arthur and Lila Weinberg (New York: Simon and Schuster, 1961), pp. 58–66. This book is a treasure for a student studying this era, as it seems to match its claim to present "the most significant magazine articles of 1902–1912." Another worth looking at is C. C. Regier, *The Era of the Muckrakers* (Gloucester, Mass.: Peter Smith, 1957). And there's an excellent bibliography on the muckrakers in *Journalism Quarterly,* XLIII (Autumn, 1966), 469–75.

21. The sense for correspondent is the one now in common usage, but the *American Thesaurus of Slang* specifies compositor: "STRING the proofs of copy set up by a piecework compositor, pasted in strips to facilitate measurement of the amount of his work," so the term may have originated in the composing room. Current citations in the World Publishing Company dictionary files show it only as meaning a newswriter.

22. Mencken, Abridged (1963), p. 739, n. 3.

23. Vol. IV, in the supplement, unnumbered pages.

24. *Editor & Publisher*, July 2, 1960.

25. M. M. Mathews, "Of Matters Lexicographical," *American Speech*, XXVIII (October, 1953), 206–7.

26. Hugo Jahn, *The Dictionary of Graphic Arts Terms* (Chicago: United Typothetae of America, 1928), p. 282.

27. Richard J. Howard, note in *Webster's New World Dictionary* file c. 1954.

28. *Editor & Publisher*, May 4, 1940, p. 36. Robb appends the note that the information was first printed in the Utica *Press* in 1932, and had been previously printed in *Editor & Publisher* in the issue for January 23, 1937.

29. "Thirty," *American Notes and Queries*, I (January, 1942), 156. The items from July 1941, p. 58, and August 1941, p. 75, were queries, idle conjecture, or repetition from the sources mentioned.

30. Correspondence to the author, March 16, 1968.

31. Cleveland *Plain Dealer*, November 29, 1959.

CHAPTER II

1. The so-called agate type used in classified advertising varies considerably in actual size.

Entry words followed by a star are discussed in Chapter I, section entitled "Origins of Some Journalism Terms."

2. The unit is used solely as a convention, and a convenient way of computing charges for advertising. In many cases, the column inch would not measure an inch on a ruler.

3. William L. Rivers, *The Mass Media* (New York: Harper and Row, Publishers, 1964), p. 42, explains the relationship of the government to AFP: "Although AFP is not subsidized directly, French government ministries pay handsomely to subscribe to its news report—an arrangement that one AFP office admitted 'could be called a disguised subsidy.'"

4. Paul P. Ashley, *Say It Safely* (Seattle: University of Washington Press, 1959), p. 36, specifies that "alleged" may not be sufficient indication of innocence in libel suits.

5. An account of the wire news services is given in Rivers, pp. 42–46.

6. Wolseley's *Understanding Magazines,* p. 95, quotes a statement from the ABC with this figure.

7. An example of use of the *backbone* would be a request from Cleveland to San Francisco for details about an accident there in which a Clevelander is involved.

8. Sources are divided almost evenly in saying 500 or 1,000 sheets; actually, it depends on what kind of paper. International Paper's *Pocket Pal* (1966), p. 175, has a table showing equivalent weights of various types.

9. Formerly a trademark, named for its inventor, Benjamin Day (1838–1916).

10. The word may not be much used in this sense, as there is some disagreement in various sources. It is given here as in Merriam-Webster's *Third Edition,* but Howard Boone Jacobson, ed., *A Mass Communications Dictionary* (New York: Philosophical Library, 1961) says "The size of type from the bottom of the descenders to the top of the ascenders, excluding leading," thus equating it with *size.* John C. Tarr, *Printing To-Day* (London: Oxford University Press, 1949) is even more perplexing: "1. top to bottom of a type, slug, lead or rule. 2. shank of type. . . ." The entry is not in other sources in this sense.

11. Only sense 1 is given in some sources, while only sense 2 is given in others. *Style Guide for Authors* (Cleveland: The World Publishing Company, 1967), p. 34, says "A page that must be turned sidewise to be read."

12. The various sources do not specify that the byline may come at the end of the story, but the author has sample pages of the San Francisco *Gater* and the Cleveland *Press* showing this style—and it is standard practice in *The New Yorker.*

13. Merriam-Webster's *Third Edition* mentions a *New York job case* as an example in its entry for *job case,* but does not have an entry for the former. Frederic S. Crispin, *Dictionary of Technical Terms* (New York: The Bruce Publishing Company, 1964) says a *New York job case* is

"a three-section case, . . . containing boxes for capitals, lower-case letters, and small capitals." This agrees with the lay of the New York job case pictured in R. Randolph Karch, *Graphic Arts Procedures* (Chicago: American Technical Society, 1948), p. 129. Karch calls this a *Yankee job case* in the index, and the two appear to be the same thing. *Glossary of Technical Terms* (Kingsport, Tennessee: Kingsport Press, Inc., 1931) describes the *Yankee job case* as "a style of type case in which the upper and lower cases of the old style news cases are combined into one case, with the lower case below or in front of the caps." Geoffrey A. Glaister, *An Encyclopedia of the Book* (Cleveland: The World Publishing Company, 1960) mentions a "space-saving set of colored plastic boxes laid out on a steel tray: it is known as the 'Rob Roy' system."

14. MacDougall has worthwhile (and amusing) discussions of trite expressions, pp. 98 and 111, while Rivers has a long list of "Trite Phrases to Avoid," pp. 103–7.

15. Glaister has devoted several pages to describing and illustrating this process in detail, with a full account of its history and usages. Most of the other sources have a simpler and more basic entry. Glaister says collotype came into use "under various names: glass printing, gelatin printing, albertype, etc." *Americana's* glossary of printing terms says that the "predominate method" of photogelatin is collotype, thus considering *photogelatin* to be the generic term. The Chicago *Manual of Style* (Chicago: The University of Chicago Press, 1961) points out that collotype is used mostly for pictorial matter.

16. Marshall Lee, *Bookmaking* (New York: R. R. Bowker Company, 1965), has a handsome set of color separations on the inside of the front cover and the end leaf. Another set may be found in *Pocket Pal* (1966), pp. 110–11.

17. There is a picture of a Columbian hand press in Lee, p. 115, complete with eagle on the top. The caption says that these presses "were still widely used at the beginning of the 20th century." Glaister also pictures this press on p. 172.

18. Margaret Nicholson, *A Manual of Copyright Practice* (New York: Oxford University Press, 1956) includes copies of copyright applications and an outline of copyright law. Copyright information is also in Irvin Graham, *Encyclopedia of Advertising* (New York: Fairchild Publications, Inc., 1952), the style manuals, and Rivers, pp. 108–14.

19. All of the illustrations in Theodore Peterson, *Magazines in the Twentieth Century* (Urbana, Illinois: University of Illinois Press, 1964) are of front covers of magazines, from the 1890's to the 1960's, a remarkable collection. There are also more of these in Mott.

20. Not the same as printing a standard halftone plate in black over a tint block. The resulting print is quite different. See illustrations of the two in *Pocket Pal* (1966), p. 108.

21. Donald D. Hoover, *"Copy!"* (New York: Thomas Y. Crowell Company, 1931) has a short chapter on "Editorial Writing," pp. 188–92, and starts by saying, "To shake up, rather than to make up, the reader's mind, has been defined as the purpose of an editorial."

22. Also called, in various sources, *end sheet, lining paper, waste leaf, waste paper, waste sheet.*

23. Century says it is "too small for letters, but used for characters of music, piece fractions, and border decorations." It was described in Merriam-Webster's *Second Edition* as "seldom used," and it is not entered in the *Third Edition* and other more recent sources.

24. As given by Hoover, and confirmed in other sources. Much has been written about this aspect of libel defense; one treatment is by Robert M. Bliss, "Fair Comment as a Defense to Libel," *Journalism Quarterly*, XLIV (Winter, 1967), 627–37.

25. Edmund C. Arnold, *Ink on Paper* (New York: Harper and Row, Publishers, 1963), p. 28, explains the origin of type family names: some are chosen by whim, or for the connotations the name may hold, as Electra, Cloister, or Futura; many are named for their designers, as Caslon,

Bodoni, Janson; others for locations, as Cheltenham; and some are intended to reflect a national characteristic, as Spartan or Scotch.

26. This also covers the corresponding area of type cast without a groove, or of wooden type.

27. A short glossary of "Journalist's Jargon" from the *New York Times* (1964) gives also as terms for filler material: *C.G.O.* or *Can Go Over, plug, punk, reserve news* and *when room*. These may be more or less internal jargon at the *Times,* as of these, only *plug* and *when room* were found in other sources. There are a great many other terms for this kind of copy; see also TIME COPY and ADVANCER.

28. Glaister has a page of illustrations of flowers and borders, p. 140; Chicago *Manual* has two pages of beautiful "Combination Flower Borders," pp. 470–71.

29. *Pocket Pal* (1966), p. 58, says it was "introduced from Europe in the middle 1920's, was known as aniline printing until 1952, when its present name was adopted."

30. Diagram showing 22 different methods of folding a folder, from 4-page to 16-page in Graham, p. 210.

31. Concept formulated by David Manning White, "The 'Gatekeeper': A Case Study in the Selection of News," *Journalism Quarterly,* XXVII (Fall, 1950), 383–90. Discussed in Schramm's *Mass Communications,* pp. 175–77.

32. Manufacturers often indicate direction of grain by underlining the pertinent dimension, as 24 x 36.

33. Arnold, *Ink on Paper,* reserves this term for "commercial intaglio printing," with a distinction between sheet-fed gravure and rotogravure. To him, gravure is always a screen process, which rules out using the term for photogravure or other variations of intalgio. Jacobson agrees with this, as does *Americana,* though the latter also says it's an abbreviation for photogravure or rotogravure. Some people in the field, as indicated in Merriam-Webster's *Third Edition* citation, have broadened the term to include several, or perhaps all, intaglio processes; the latter gives "drypoint, mezzotint, burin engraving and all forms of etching." Glaister equates the term with intaglio. Some

sources enter a sense as a shortened form of photogravure, and others mention "copper or wooden plates."

34. Marjorie E. Skillin, *et al., Words Into Type* (New York: Appleton-Century-Crofts, 1964), p. 113, says paragraphs set in this way are called *flush-and-hang paragraphs,* and Graham, p. 336, enters this term as *overhanging indention.*

35. MacDougall discusses this form, p. 52ff. On page 55 he says, "for more than a half-century, this has been the orthodox form of news writing."

36. One of the terms the author has "always" known, without memory of where it was first heard. It is in Merriam-Webster's *Third Edition.* Mencken, Suppl. II, p. 766, gives this, with alternate *lens-hog,* and it was noticed in the *Cleveland Press* in January, 1968, as *lens lizard.* Not in other common sources, including slang dictionaries or the *Dictionary of Americanisms.*

37. Shramm, pp. 5–7, gives a helpful and interesting chronology of the developments of mass communications. See also Rivers' Chapter 2, "The Network of Mass Communications."

38. An excellent digest of studies on the effects of mass media is given by Jacobson in his introduction; an extensive selection of readings is provided in Schramm, and the whole of Rivers' *The Mass Media* is worthy of notice.

39. Claims have been put forth that movable type was invented by Larens Janszoon Coster (or Koster) of Haarlem, Netherlands, c. 1440, but the claims were never substantiated.

40. See Note 20, Chapter I, above.

41. Some sources give the main entry for this term at *typeholder.* Homer Chagnon, at the bindery of World Publishing Company, says the two words may be used interchangeably. He also points out that this operation is done by machine nowadays, but there is enough incidental hand binding done to keep these tools in use.

42. A list of standard paper sizes is given in George S. Brady, *Materials Handbook* (New York: McGraw-Hill,

Inc., 1963), p. 888. See also *Pocket Pal* (1966), p. 179, or Lee, p. 137.

The names of paper sizes are something else again. Tarr gives the names of paper sizes in his glossary. The Kingsport glossary, p. 153, also has the list of names of paper sizes, as does Glaister, p. 298. *The Dictionary of Paper* (New York: American Paper and Pulp Association, 1940), pp. 303–306, has a comprehensive coverage, with English and American nomenclature listed for all kinds and sizes of paper.

43. Arnold, in *Ink on Paper*, p. 231, describes this as a fine-arts hand-printing process, says that no more than 500 prints a day may be produced.

44. Mencken, Suppl. II, p. 766, says first used (he believes) by *Variety*.

45. Sense 3 is given in *Americana's* glossary and Jacobson, but is not in Merriam-Webster's *Third Edition*. The term is relatively new, and is not yet in very common usage. The *Oxford English Dictionary's* first citation (for *planographic*) is 1897, and *planograph* was not documented until 1928. The *Dictionary of Americanisms* and Mencken do not enter the term. A glossary given in the *New York Times* in 1965 gives it as a synonym for offset lithography.

46. One of the most popular printers' marks through the centuries has been the orb-and-cross. An illustration of 30 variations of this may be found in Douglas C. McMurtrie, *The Book* (New York: Oxford University Press, 1943), p. 293.

47. A relatively new concept, first brought to public attention in 1890. Ashley devotes Chapter 14 to the right of privacy. MacDougall discusses "Invasion of Privacy" briefly but well, p. 26. See also Rivers, p. 119, and Robert Strunsky, "The Invasion of Privacy (5)," *The American Scholar*, XXIX (Spring, 1960), 219–26.

48. Nicholson, pp. 147–49, discusses the concept of public domain.

49. An excellent comprehensive chart of book sizes is given in Merriam-Webster's *Third Edition*. Glaister lists comparable English and American sizes, pp. 39, 40. The Chicago *Manual* lists book sizes, p. 265; and Skillin discusses them, p. 104ff.

50. An excellent short summary of various readability formulas is given in Wolseley's *Understanding Magazines*, pp. 147–49.

51. In few sources; Arnold's treatment in *Ink on Paper*, p. 306, is the most helpful.

52. From a letter from Harold T. Kent, Jr., San Francisco Bureau of UPI: REPORT—This refers basically to the service we give the newspapers. At the beginning of each new cycle on the wire, this advisory to editors is moved: 'Editors: The UPI report for morning/afternoon papers begins.' The word 'report' refers to everything that will move on that wire during the next 12 hours. There are two cycles a day, one for morning papers and one for afternoon papers. Each cycle begins at 1 o'clock EST. It begins with an editor's schedule, which lists all the important stories that will be moved. All these stories plus whatever features and breaking stories move makes up that day's 'report.' " January 19, 1968.

53. Graham cross-refers to *Fairchild Photo-electric engraver*, and there gives an excellent description of the apparatus.

54. Fine account of the halftone process, with illustrations of the screen, can be found in Lee, p. 110; in Arnold's *Ink on Paper*, p. 162ff.; Glaister, p. 369ff.; and *Pocket Pal* (1966), pp. 106–109.

55. The *Oxford English Dictionary's* first citation for this usage in 1749; the OED entry is labeled "rare," so apparently the usage fell into disfavor for a time.

56. Arnold, *Ink on Paper*, explains this process was developed by WPA Federal Arts Project in the thirties, and tells of its extensive commercial applications, pp. 232–34.

57. *Oxford English Dictionary's* first citation is 1871.

58. The *New York Times'* "Times Talk" list of Journalist's Jargon says that at the *Times,* a take is "approximately 60 lines of classified ad copy. . . ."

59. The glossary of Thomas E. Berry, *Journalism Today* (Philadelphia: Chilton Company, 1958) points out that the thumbnail illustration should never be placed on the margin edge of a column, but this rule is unknown or ignored by many publications. They do, however, usually stick to another admonition that the thumbnail cut should be placed in the upper part of the story.

60. See Note 20, above.

61. Sources vary widely. First they differ on what to call the major division. Arnold chooses *race;* the Chicago *Manual* calls them *styles;* Lee and Skillin prefer *class;* Glaister says *group;* and many dictionaries and graphic arts books say *design.*

What to put within each grouping causes more disagreement. We have chosen Arnold's for the entry in this book. Skillin and Chicago also have five classifications: "roman, italic, script, gothic, and text." Lee has four: "roman, abstract (sans serif and block [square] serif), cursive (including the italic form of roman), and decorative." Glaister (British) says: "venetian, old face, modern, and jobbing, each with their respective italics. See also exotic types, . . ."

62. An excellent explanation of this, and examples, can be found in Skillin, pp. 86, 87; and can be seen by comparing type specimens in the Chicago *Manual* or any type specimen book.

63. See Rivers, pp. 42–46, for information about wire news services.

64. A *New York Times* glossary, May 23, 1965, points out that the web of paper fed into a rotary press is "printed, and most often, folded, pasted, and counted in one continuous operation."

Sources Consulted

TRADITIONAL SOURCES

The first source for English words is, of course, the *Oxford English Dictionary*. Its wealth of dated citations and painstaking etymologies impart an immeasurable warmth to the researcher's heart, especially if he consults sparser sources before he turns to the old standby. Nearly as valuable is the *Century Dictionary*. It has its differences, yet its scholarship is as painstaking as the OED. Though it leaves out dates on its citations and has fewer of them, therefore limiting its value in one dimension, it has beautiful typography, over 10,000 illustrations, and a great deal more detail in technical entries and those having to do with natural history than does the OED. Book design was the responsibility of Theodore Low De Vinne (1828–1914), noted especially for fine wood engravings and halftones. He also designed the Book of Common Prayer, and founded the Grolier Club.

But neither of these basic sources deal exhaustively with compound terms, which take a rather astounding amount of space in the more modern dictionaries. And they are general, not specialized—they do not go into the fine points, of, for example, printing methods. Therefore, while the huge OED and *Century Dictionary* may be understood as being the basic sources consulted for many entries in the glossary, they serve as background rather than the foreground that is today.

MODERN GENERAL SOURCES

The most easily available ready reference has been *Webster's New World Dictionary*, because of the author's editorial connection with it. Also used were *Merriam-Webster's Second* and *Third New International Dictionaries, The World Book Dictionary* and its companion *World Book*

Encyclopedia, and *The Random House Dictionary. The Columbia Encyclopedia,* the *Encyclopedia Americana,* the *Encyclopaedia Britannica,* and the *Universal Standard Encyclopedia* have also been consulted frequently. For British terms, there have been *Cassell's English Dictionary,* and the *Penguin Dictionary of English* with its *Penguin Encyclopedia.* All of these are identified more fully in the bibliography, along with a more complete listing of all material consulted.

SPECIALIZED SOURCES

GRAPHIC ARTS

The most generally satisfactory glossary of printing terms consulted has been that produced by the Kingsport Press in Tennessee, a *Glossary of Technical Terms,* in 1931. It contains not only a wealth of printing terms, but biographical entries for notable bookbinders and type designers, and trademarks for binding cloth, paper, etc. Unfortunately, it is out of print, and cannot be considered up-to-date. Shorter, but in all ways as valuable (in some cases, more so) in the terms that are entered, is the glossary of graphic arts terms in the *Encyclopedia Americana.* The source from which these terms were taken is a *Dictionary of Graphic Arts,* published in 1957 by "Printing Industry of America, the Education Council, and the Research and Engineering Council of the Graphic Arts Industry," which contains 10,000 entries.

The field of graphic arts has been thoroughly covered, and the present-day writer who sets out to prepare a compilation of graphic arts terms will find a great deal of source material for his endeavor, but he may not find much of a market for still another book on the graphic arts when he has finished. It will need to have a special slant, or be aimed at a specific group.

The able work of R. Randolph Karch has shown up in several works. The glossary of his own book, *Printing and the Allied Trades,* contains an excellent listing of printing, copying, and photographic devices and machines by trade names. These are in addition to conventional printing terms, also covered in Karch's glossary in his *Graphic Arts Procedures.*

Arnold's *Ink on Paper,* its glossary, chapter on printing terms, and other material throughout, has been most valuable. An excellent little book is *Pocket Pal,* printed by the International Paper Company. The entire contents are fine, and the glossary of graphic arts terms, though necessarily abridged, was useful. Both the 1963 and 1966 editions were used, with the glossary brought up to date in the later edition. Also of considerable scope is Hugo Jahn's *Dictionary of Graphic Arts Terms,* 1928—again, slightly outdated.

General technical dictionaries that contain a large number of printing terms were also consulted. Among these are Flood & West's *Dictionary of Scientific and Technical Words;* and Frederic S. Crispin's *Dictionary of Technical Terms* (1940 and 1966 editions were both used; again, the latter was brought up to date with the addition of some photographic and electronic terms).

The popular stylebooks have glossaries of printing terms, as well as other information: Skillins' *Words Into Type, The Government Printing Office Style Manual,* and the University of Chicago *Manual of Style* have been consulted and respected.

ADVERTISING

The most remarkable work on advertising terms is Irvin Graham's *Encyclopedia of Advertising* (1952), a 606-page volume of ". . . more than 1100 entries relating to Advertising, Marketing, Publishing, Public Relations, Publicity and the Graphic Arts, combined with valuable reference material. . . ." The long, chatty entries, with everything from statistics on the "Age-Group Penetration (Among All Match Users)" [at the entry for *Match Books*] to a directory of advertising associations, comprise a treasury of information for the advertising student. Advertising terms were also checked in H. Victor Grohmann's *Advertising Terminology*. Grohmann was also associate editor of *A Mass Communications Dictionary*, which contains a considerable number of entries for advertising.

NEWSPAPER AND MAGAZINE

Newspaper and magazine terms were gathered from a wide selection of sources. Among them were glossaries in MacDougall's *Interpretative Reporting*, Arnold's *Functional Newspaper Design*, two that appeared in the *New York Times*, a chapter in Hoover's *"Copy!"*, entitled "Why Do We Talk Like That?", Mills' glossary from Wolseley's *The Magazine World*, and Jacobi's glossary from Wolseley's *Understanding Magazines*.

BOOK PRODUCTION

Terms having to do with book production were explored with great pleasure in Lee's *Bookmaking*, and Glaister's *Encyclopedia of the Book*. One hesitates to recommend the latter, as it appears to be now out of print, or at least unavailable through its American distributor, World Publish-

ing Company. This is a great loss. It is British, and uses
the British spellings and words, as *forme* for *form, fount*
for *font,* and *ruby* for *agate.* All of this, of course, adds a
little flavor, but its chief charm lies in its illustrations,
nearly too good and perfect to be true. The most handsome are those illustrating each kind of printing process.
Glaister also has a considerable number of biographical
entries for printers, inventors of printing devices and
machines, and for noted bibliophiles. Lee's definitions and
explanations are excellent, too. Its illustrations are of a
different kind, with sketches in the book margins, but just
as helpful and handsome. Several trips to the bindery of
the World Publishing Company and conversations with
personnel were helpful, as were the author's personal ad-
ventures in bookbinding at the Graphic Arts Center for
employees of World Publishing Company.

LAW OF THE PRESS

Legal terms were sought in a variety of sources, as Ashley's
Say It Safely, Nicholson's *A Manual of Copyright Practice,*
Black's Law Dictionary, and *Bouvier's Law Dictionary.*
Graham's *Encyclopedia of Advertising* also gives attention
to legal terminology.

PAPER

Terms having to do with paper were available in several
of the sources already named, including International
Paper Company's *Pocket Pal,* but one book deserves special
mention. *The Dictionary of Paper,* published by the American Paper and Pulp Association in 1940, is a remarkable
piece of work. The scope is nearly unimaginable, number
of entries remarkably high for the subject, and workmanship seems above reproach. It was compiled by a com-

mittee of 14 members, disproving the old saw that a committee can never accomplish anything.

PHOTOGRAPHY

An excellent reference for photographic terms is *Military Standardization Handbook Glossary of Photographic Terms Including Document Reproduction,* published by the Department of the Army, the Navy, and the Air Force in 1961. It appears to be quite comprehensive. Terms having to do with photography were also available in several of the books and glossaries heretofore mentioned, especially those for graphic arts.

SLANG

The words regarded as "jargon" or slang were culled from a great many sources, including nearly all of those named to this point. Then there were also Mathews' *A Dictionary of Americanisms, A Dictionary of American English,* Wentworth's *American Dialect Dictionary,* Pyles' *Words and Ways of American English,* Mencken's *The American Language,* Wentworth and Flexner's *Dictionary of American Slang,* Weingarten's *An American Dictionary of Slang,* and Berrey and Van den Bark's *The American Thesaurus of Slang.* Help on these terms was obtained from conversation and correspondence with practicing journalists also, as Harold Kent of United Press International, and some of the members of Theta Sigma Phi professional chapter in Cleveland.

MASS COMMUNICATIONS

A work of much interest during the compiling of this glossary has been *A Mass Communications Dictionary*, edited by Howard Boone Jacobson. It is relatively new (1961), modern, and comparable to this glossary of print-communications terms, with significant differences. It is a combined effort: graphic arts terms were from Karch, advertising terms by Grohmann, with other fields handled by 19 or 20 contributing editors or organizations.

Jacobson has given considerable attention to the electronic media. His entries for motion pictures and photography seem to be comprehensive, with television and radio running a close second. The book should be valuable to radio-television majors. Also especially notable is a large number of entries having to do with outdoor advertising, principally billboards. This may be the most comprehensive source on this particular field. There are also many entries concerning newspaper distribution and subscriptions, contributed by the Audit Bureau of Circulations.

OTHER SOURCES OF INFORMATION

The books mentioned to this point were constantly available, and most of them open, during the period when the glossary of print-communications terms was put together. Notes appended to the glossary indicate disagreements and perplexities within and about entries in these sources, but by and large, they have been respected. The books were augmented by more specialized reference sources from the Editorial Services, Art, and Encyclopedia Departments at World Publishing Company; from the stupendous collection at the Cleveland Public Library; and a constant flow of material provided by friends and relatives.

In addition to these books and people, another invaluable source of information has been used, one not available to the ordinary researcher—the citation files of current usage of terms in the Dictionary Department of World Publishing Company. It is with much gratitude that I have consulted these files in working on this glossary. Seeing anywhere from ten to over a hundred clippings from various sources in which a term is actually used can give the lexicographer a fine perspective. The citation files not only show new terms just coming into usage, but also old ones used in new ways, or occasionally, indications that a once-used word has fallen into disuse. This latters occurs through lack of citations, or more often, by a slowing down by date. A term that may have wide usage at one time may have gone out of vogue almost entirely within a few years.

Bibliography

With Some Annotations

Adeline's Art Dictionary. New York: D. Appleton-Century Company, Inc., 1937.

Allen, Charles Laurel. *The Journalist's Manual of Printing*. New York: Thomas Nelson & Sons, 1929.

Allen, Eric W. *Printing for the Journalist*. New York: Alfred A. Knopf, Inc., 1928. Quite outdated.

Arnold, Edmund C. *Functional Newspaper Design*. New York: Harper and Row, Publishers, 1956. Glossary, pp. 327–37.

————. *Ink on Paper*. New York: Harper and Row, Publishers, 1963. Glossary, pp. 290–313.

Ashley, Paul P. *Say It Safely*. Seattle: University of Washington Press, 1959.

Auerbach, Len. "Radio Glossary." *U.S. Radio,* V (March, 1961). A five-page glossary of "radio terms, compiled by Ohio Stations Representatives, Cleveland, . . . intended as a guide of most-used or most-referred-to terms in radio advertising."

Barnett, Lincoln. *The Treasure of Our Tongue*. New York: Alfred A. Knopf, Inc., 1964.

Barron, John N. *The Language of Painting, an Informal Dictionary*. Cleveland: The World Publishing Company, 1967.

Bent, Silas. *Newspaper Crusaders, A Neglected Story*. New York: McGraw-Hill, Inc., 1939. Records the role of the newspapers from the beginning of our history in their crusading efforts; parallels books written about magazine muckrakers.

Berry, Lester V., and Van den Bark, Melvin. *The American Thesaurus of Slang*. 2nd ed. New York: Thomas Y. Crowell Company, 1953.

Berry, Thomas Elliott. *Journalism Today*. Philadelphia: Chilton Company, 1958. Glossary, pp. 469–87. Berry was one of the consultants for *A Mass Communications Dictionary*.

Black, Henry Campbell. *Black's Law Dictionary*. 4th ed. St. Paul, Minn.: West Publishing Company, 1951.

Bliss, Robert M. "Fair Comment as a Defense to Libel." *Journalism Quarterly*, XLIV (Winter, 1967), 627–37.

Bouvier's Law Dictionary. Edited by William Edward Baldwin. Cleveland: Banks-Baldwin Law Publishing Company, 1948.

Brady, George S. *Materials Handbook*. 9th ed. New York: McGraw-Hill, Inc., 1963.

Campbell, Laurence R., and Wolseley, Roland E. *How to Report and Write the News*. Englewood Cliffs, New Jersey: Prentice-Hall, Inc., 1961. Glossary, pp. 565–70.

———. *Newsmen at Work*. Boston: Houghton Mifflin Company, 1949. Glossary, pp. 525–28.

Carpenter, Edward. *A House of Kings, The Official History of Westminster Abbey*. New York: The John Day Company, 1966.

Cassell's English Dictionary. London: Cassell and Company, Ltd., 1962.

Century Dictionary and Cyclopedia, The. 12 vols. New York: The Century Company, 1913.

Chambers's Technical Dictionary. 3rd ed. Edited by C. F. Tweney and L. E. C. Hughes. New York: The Macmillan Company, 1967.

Clark, Donald T., and Gottfried, Bert A. *Dictionary of Business and Finance*. New York: Thomas Y. Crowell Company, 1957.

Clark, Wesley C., ed. *Journalism Tomorrow*. Syracuse: Syracuse University Press, 1958.

Collier's Encyclopedia. 24 vols. n.p.: Crowell Collier and Macmillan, Inc., 1967.

Collins, Charles. "Approved Theory for Origin of '30,'" from column "A Line o' Type or Two." *Chicago Tribune*, January 16, 1940, p. 10.

———. "Origin of Thirty," from column "A Line o' Type or Two." *Chicago Tribune*, January 13, 1940, p. 10.

———. "Seven Theories About 30," from column "A Line o' Type or Two." *Chicago Tribune,* January 15, 1940, p. 10.

Collins, F. Howard. *Authors' & Printers' Dictionary.* 7th ed. London: Humphrey Milford, 1933.

Columbia Encyclopedia, The. New York: Columbia University Press, 1964.

Committee on Modern Journalism [57 coauthors listed]. *Modern Journalism.* New York: Pitman Publishing Corporation, 1962.

Crispin, Frederic S. *Dictionary of Technical Terms.* 3rd ed. New York: The Bruce Publishing Company, 1940; also 10th ed., 1964.

Dictionary of American English, A. 4 vols. Chicago: The University of Chicago Press, 1938.

Dictionary of Electronic Terms. 7th ed. Chicago: Allied Radio Corporation, 1963. Sub-title: "Concise definitions of words used in radio, television and electronics."

Dictionary of Paper, The. New York: American Paper and Pulp Association, 1940.

Encyclopaedia Britannica. 24 vols. Chicago: Encyclopaedia Britannica, 1957.

Encyclopedia Americana, The. 30 vols. New York: Americana Corporation, 1957.

Ferguson, Rowena. *Editing the Small Magazine.* New York: Columbia University Press, 1958.

Flood W. E., and West, Michael. *Dictionary of Scientific and Technical Words.* 2nd ed. London: Longmans, Green and Company, 1953.

Follett, Wilson. *Modern American Usage.* New York: Hill & Wang, 1966.

Fowler, H. W. *A Dictionary of Modern English Usage.* Oxford: Oxford University Press, 1965.

Glaister, Geoffrey Ashall. *An Encyclopedia of the Book*. Cleveland: The World Publishing Company, 1960. The title page says: "Terms used in Paper-Making, Printing, Bookbinding and Publishing, with Notes on Illuminated Manuscripts, Bibliophiles, Private Presses and Printing Societies. Including Illustrations and Translated Extracts from *Grafisk Uppslagsbok* (Esselte, Stockholm)." The book is printed in Great Britain.

Glossary of Technical Terms. Kingsport, Tennessee: Kingsport Press, Inc., 1931. The best source for graphic arts terms.

Golden, Hal, and Hanson, Kitty. *Working with the Working Press*. Dobbs Ferry, New York: Oceana Publications, Inc., 1962. Glossary, pp. 210–22.

Gorder, L. O., ed. *A Dictionary of Radio Terms*. Chicago: Allied Radio Corporation, 1943.

Graham, E. C., ed. *The Basic Dictionary of Science*. New York: The Macmillan Company, 1966. A British book, helpful for photographic terms.

Graham, Irvin. *Encyclopedia of Advertising*. New York: Fairchild Publications, Inc., 1952.

Gress, Edmund G. *The Art & Practice of Typography*. New York: Oswald Publishing Company, 1917. A handsome old book, full of intriguing illustrations.

Grohmann, Victor H. *Advertising Terminology*. New York: Needham and Grohmann, Inc., 1952.

Haber, Tom Burns. "Canine Terms Applied to Human Beings: II." *American Speech*, XL (December, 1965), 255. The term "bulldog edition" appears here, with its definition, but with no explanation of its origin. Also "hound's teeth" for "river."

Heflin, Woodford Agee, ed. *The United States Air Force Dictionary*. Washington, D.C.: Air University Press, 1956. Helpful for terms in photography, and for a remarkably comprehensive selection of abbreviations, in many fields.

Hoover, Donald D. *"Copy!"* New York: Thomas Y. Crowell Company, 1931.

Irwin, Will. *Propaganda and the News.* New York: Mc-Graw-Hill, Inc., 1936.

Jacobson, Howard Boone, ed. *A Mass Communications Dictionary.* New York: Philosophical Library, 1961.
Jahn, Hugo. *The Dictionary of Graphic Arts Terms.* Chicago: United Typothetae of America, 1928.

Kansas City Star. "Graphic Arts: Kansas City," Section J, January 14, 1968.
Karch, R. Randolph, *Graphic Arts Procedures.* Chicago: American Technical Society, 1948. Glossary, pp. 345–61.
———. *Printing and the Allied Trades.* New York: Pitman Publishing Corporation, 1962.
Kempner, Stanley. *Television Encyclopedia.* New York: Fairchild Publishing Company, 1948.

Lee, Marshall. *Bookmaking.* New York: R. R. Bowker Company, 1965.

MacDougall, Curtis D. *Interpretative Reporting.* 4th ed. New York: The Macmillan Company, 1963. Glossary, pp. 511–14.
Manly, Harold P. *Drake's Radio-Television Electronic Dictionary.* Chicago: Frederick J. Drake and Company, 1956.
Manual of Style, A. 11th ed. Chicago: The University of Chicago Press, 1949; 1961 impression. Glossary, pp. 245–72.
Mathews, Mitford M. *A Dictionary of Americanisms.* 2 vols. Chicago: The University of Chicago Press, 1951.
———. "Of Matters Lexicographical." *American Speech,* XXVIII (October, 1953), 206–7.
Mayberry, George, ed. *A Concise Dictionary of Abbreviations.* New York: Tudor Publishing Company, 1961.

McGraw-Hill Encyclopedia of Science and Technology. 15 vols. McGraw-Hill Inc., 1960.

McMurtrie, Douglas C. *The Book.* New York: Oxford University Press, 1943.

Mencken, H. L. *The American Language.* New York: Alfred A. Knopf, Inc., 1936; Suppl. I, 1945; Suppl. II, 1948; Abridged, 1963.

Military Standardization Handbook, Glossary of Photographic Terms Including Document Reproduction. Washington, D. C.: Department of the Army, 1961. From the information inside, it appears that the glossary was prepared jointly by the Departments of the Army, the Navy, and the Air Force.

Miller, Thomas H., and Brummitt, Wyatt. *This is Photography.* Garden City, New York: Garden City Books, 1959.

Mott, Frank Luther. *American Journalism: A History: 1690–1960.* 3rd ed. New York: The Macmillan Company, 1963.

————. *A History of American Magazines.* Cambridge, Mass.: Harvard University Press, 1957. Packed full of a remarkable amount of information. Many fascinating illustrations.

New York Times. "Journalists' Jargon," from *Times Talk,* XVII (April, 1964), 12. This publication is a house organ. The one-page glossary has 64 terms defined; some terms were not found elsewhere, and were therefore rather assumed to be the *Times'* own jargon.

————. "The World of the Printed Word: a Reader's Glossary," section entitled "The Information Revolution," May 23, 1965, p. 13.

Nicholson, Margaret. *A Manual of Copyright Practice.* New York: Oxford University Press, 1956.

Otto, William N., and Finney, Nat S. *Headlines and By-Lines.* New York: Harcourt, Brace and Company, 1946. Glossary, pp. 439–45.

Oxford English Dictionary, The. 12 vols. and Supplement. London: Oxford University Press, 1933. Originally entitled *A New English Dictionary on Historical Principles.* The actual editing of this work took from 1878 until 1928. The history of the dictionary, as told in its Introduction, excites admiration for the "harmless drudges" that labored so many years to put together this record of our language.

Penguin Dictionary of English, The. Harmondsworth, Middlesex, England: Penguin Books Ltd., 1965.

Penguin Encyclopedia, The. Harmondsworth, Middlesex, England: Penguin Books Ltd., 1965.

Peterson, Theodore. *Magazines in the Twentieth Century.* Urbana, Illinois: University of Illinois Press, 1964. Covers the period from the 1890's to 1964. Illustrations are all magazine covers, a fine selection.

Plain Dealer Sunday Magazine. "This is Rotogravure," March 5, 1967, pp. 56–63.

Pocket Pal. 7th ed. New York: International Paper Company, 1963; also 9th ed., 1966. Jacobson's *A Mass Communications Dictionary,* p. xii, says that *Pocket Pal* is by R. A. Faulkner, but the name does not appear in the book itself. We can assume the information is correct, however, as Faulkner was one of the consultants for *A Mass Communications Dictionary.*

Porte, R. T. *Dictionary of Printing Terms.* Salt Lake City, Utah: The Porte Press, 1941.

Price, Frank James. "Journalism Enrollments Hit New High at 24,445." *Journalism Quarterly,* XLIV (Winter, 1967), 812.

Pyles, Thomas. *Words and Ways of American English.* New York: Random House, Inc., 1952.

Random House Dictionary, The. [unabridged] New York: Random House, Inc., 1967.

Regier, C. C. *The Era of the Muckrakers*. Gloucester, Mass.: Peter Smith, Publisher, 1957. Bibliography, pp. 217–41.

Rittenhouse, Mignon. *The Amazing Nellie Bly*. New York: E. P. Dutton & Company, Inc., 1956.

Rivers, William L. *Finding Facts, A Research Manual for Journalists*. New York: Magazine Publishers Association, Inc., 1966.

———. *The Mass Media*. New York: Harper and Row, Publishers, 1964. An excellent work, with a wealth of material.

Robb, Arthur. "Shop Talk at Thirty." *Editor & Publisher,* May 4, 1940, p. 36.

Runes, Dagobert D., and Shrickel, Harry G., eds. *Encyclopedia of the Arts*. New York: Philosophical Library, 1946.

Schramm, Wilbur, ed. *Mass Communications*. Urbana, Illinois: University of Illinois Press, 1960.

Schwarzlose, Richard A. "United States Newspapers' Wire Service Resources." *Journalism Quarterly*, XLIII (Winter, 1966), 629ff.

Scott's Specialized Catalogue of United States Stamps. 40th ed. Edited by Gordon R. Harmer and Eugene N. Costales. New York: Scott Publications, 1962. Several sections discuss printing processes. Our postage stamps constitute some of the finest printing specimens in America.

Skillin, Marjorie E., Gay, Robert M., *et al. Words Into Type*. New York: Appleton-Century-Crofts, 1964. Glossary, pp. 538–48.

Stoutenburgh, John L., Jr. *Dictionary of Arts and Crafts*. New York: Philosophical Library, 1956.

Stranger, Ralph (pseud.). *Dictionary of Radio and Television Terms*. Brooklyn: Chemical Publishing Company, 1941.

Strunsky, Robert. "The Invasion of Privacy (5)." *The American Scholar,* XXIX (Spring, 1960), 219–26. One of a series of five articles on the invasion of privacy; the other authors were Richard H. Rovere, August Heckscher, Granville Hicks, and Gerald W. Johnson.

Style Guide for Authors. [No author named.] Cleveland: The World Publishing Company, 1967. Glossary, pp. 33–41. A house publication, available only to World authors and editors.

Tarr, John C. *Printing To-Day.* London: Oxford University Press, 1949.

"Thirty." *American Notes and Queries,* I (July, 1941), 58; (August, 1941), 75; and (January, 1942), 156.

Turnbull, Arthur T., and Baird, Russell N. *The Graphics of Communication.* New York: Holt, Rinehart and Winston, Inc., 1964. Glossary, pp. 321–32.

United States Government Printing Office. *Style Manual.* Washington, D.C., 1959; also Revised Edition, 1967.

Universal Standard Encyclopedia, The. 36 vols. New York: Unicorn Publishers, Inc., 1955.

Van Nostrand's Scientific Encyclopedia. 3rd ed. Princeton, N.J.: D. Van Nostrand Company, Inc., 1958.

Webster's New International Dictionary, Second Edition. Springfield, Mass.: G. and C. Merriam Company, 1952.

Webster's New International Dictionary, Third Edition. Springfield, Mass.: G. and C. Merriam Company, 1964; also 1961 printing. There were many changes in the later printing. Name on title page is *Webster's Third New International Dictionary,* but it is often given as above in order to correspond with the Second Edition.

Webster's New World Dictionary of the American Language. Cleveland: The World Publishing Company, 1966.

Weinberg, Arthur and Lila, eds. *The Muckrakers*. New York: Simon and Schuster, Inc., 1961.

Weingarten, Joseph A. *An American Dictionary of Slang*. New York: By the Author, 1954.

Wentworth, Harold. *American Dialect Dictionary*. New York: Thomas Y. Crowell Company, 1944.

————, and Flexner, Stuart Berg. *Dictionary of American Slang*. New York: Thomas Y. Crowell Company, 1960; also Supplemented Edition, 1967.

Wheelwright, William Bond. *Paper Trade Terms, a Glossary for the Allied Trades*. Boston: The Callaway Associates, 1951.

White, David Manning. "The 'Gatekeeper': A Case Study in the Selection of News." *Journalism Quarterly*, XXVII (Fall, 1950), 383–90.

Wolseley, Roland E. *The Magazine World*. New York: Prentice-Hall, Inc., 1955. Glossary, pp. 381–89, compiled by Sally M. Mills.

————. *Understanding Magazines*. Ames, Iowa: The Iowa State University Press, 1965. Glossary, pp. 419–31, compiled by Ronna Ann Jacobi.

Woodward, Helen. *The Lady Persuaders*. New York: Ivan Obolensky, Inc., 1960. Women's magazines from 1828 to 1959. An excellent survey, with a few fine illustrations, artfully chosen.

World Almanac, The. New York: Newspaper Enterprise Association, Inc., 1968; also 1966 and 1967.

World Book Dictionary, The. Chicago: Thorndike-Barnhart Dictionary Series, Doubleday & Company, Inc., 1962.

World Book Encyclopedia, The. 20 vols. Chicago: Field Enterprises Educational Corporation, 1966.

This book is set in 10-point Century Expanded roman type, with its companion italic, on a 12-point body. The type was designed around 1900 by the American inventor, printer, and type designer, Linn Boyd Benton.

The title page is in 18-point and 14-point News Gothic Bold. Chapter headings are in 14-point News Gothic Bold. This type originated with the American Type Founders in 1908, and was designed by Morris Fuller Benton.

The book was printed and bound by Book Graphics, Inc., Evanston, Illinois 60201.